International Real Estate Investments:

A Comparative Study between Housing
Markets in Europe and the U.S.

International Real Estate Investments:

A Comparative Study between Housing Markets in Europe and the U.S.

KIM SCHEURINGER

Manufacture and publishing: BoD- Books on Demand, Norderstedt

Approved on Application by Prof. Dr. Roland Füss
project thesis

University of St.Gallen
School of Management, Economics, Law and Social Sciences (HSG)
Dufourstrasse 50, 9000 St.Gallen, Switzerland

First published in 2021
Copyright @ Kim Scheuringer
Paperback ISBN: 978-3-7534-9595-8

Bibliografische Information der Deutschen Nationalbibliothek: Die
Deutsche Nationalbibliothek verzeichnet diese Publikation in der
Deutschen Nationalbibliografie; detaillierte bibliografische Daten
sind im Internet über dnb.dnb.de abrufbar.

Acknowledgements

Special thanks should be given to Robert Füss, whose expertise was invaluable in setting up the framework and methodology and for his ongoing professional guidance as well as to all of the staff at HSG for the useful and constructive support.

I would like to express my very great appreciation to Janine Lange, Araceli Fancher-Ferreira and Dietmar Horst for editing and their valuable insights.

CARE diagnostica deserves special thanks for financial support and providing insight into the financial world as well as to Mr. Masaki Nishinaga for his valuable recommendation.

I could not have completed this dissertation without the support of Emily Cirotzki.

Finally, Noah, Nils und Nelio Horeis provided stimulating discussions as well as happy distractions to rest my mind outside of my research.

MANAGEMENT SUMMARY

Purpose – The purpose of this work is to build a case for investing in international real estate focusing on single-family homes. In so doing, the comparative study takes into consideration transaction costs, taxation, as well as regulation and other institutional settings.

Design / methodology / approach – In this study average and total returns of a 20-year investment in four representative markets - Germany, Spain, San Diego, and Dallas – on two continents are compared against the general stock and bond markets. Volatility considerations are discussed, and their impact on return is shown. Risks are assessed as well as strategies for its reduction are provided. Finally, a concluding recommendation of where to invest is provided.

Empirical findings – At 4.63 % and 4.75 %, respectively, annual returns after inflation for San Diego and Dallas single family home investments are found in-line with world stock returns at 4.80 %. At 3.87 % the Spanish market follows closely behind eclipsing German real estate with 1.50 % and bonds at 1.48 %. Limited correlation among the markets and amongst the asset classes allow for risk minimization by diversification.

Practical implications – The results suggest that real estate in particular in the San Diego area of California is a suitable target both in terms of return and safety, especially for long-term horizons. When focusing on Europe, the Spanish real estate market looks attractive for investors. The remaining capital should be allocated into international stocks via mutual funds linked to the MSCI world index.

Originality / value – The study adds additional insight on investments strategies into the mainly untouched area of single-family real estate returns on different continents and markets.

TABLE OF CONTENTS

Table of Contents

TABLES AND FIGURES

LIST OF ABBREVATIONS

BIS	Bank for International Settlements, Basel
CPA	Certified Public Accountant
ETF	Exchange Traded Fund
FED	Federal Reserve System
FTSE	FTSE Group, London
FX	Foreign Exchange Market
HOA	Homeowner Association
IBI	Impuesto sobre Bienes Inmuebles
INE	Instituto Nacional de Estadística, Madrid
JLL	Jones Lang LaSalle, Chicago
MSCI	MSCI Inc., New York
NYSE	New York Stock Exchange
REIT	Real Estate Investment Trust
ROI	Return on Investment
SEC	United States Securities and Exchange Commission

I. INTRODUCTION

Beyond the scarifying task to earn money for the living more than a little fortune may be left for safeguarding the own or the relative's financial future for the years to come. For long, investments and strategies thereof have been used, discussed, thought after and extensively analyzed (Edwards, 1906; Bowen, 1989; Graham, 1949; Hur, 2020).

"A hundred Zuz in business, and everyday meat and wine; a hundred Zuz in land, and salt and vegetables" (Talmud, 200, D. 463) translated to *"Let every man divide his money into three parts, and invest a third in land, a third in business and a third let him keep by him in reserve."* (Ycombinator, 2020) can be read in the Talmud of the year 200.

The second part, the "land" deserves more attention as real estate (Goddard, 2012, p. 1-6) – notably the single-family housing market - often is only seen as having a "roof over the head" or being a financial, inflation-shielded security rather than a return generating asset. Even more rarely buying a house seems to be judged against other forms of investments.

In our globalized world buying houses is not limited to the hometown or country. Like stocks and bonds, real estate investment opportunities are available across all continents around the world. Focusing on a Western investor the scope is narrowed down towards Europe and the North America, in particular Western Europe and the United States where four examples of housing markets are presented – Germany, Spain, the San Diego metro area of California and Dallas in Texas. Each with its own characteristics, these regions represent different role models satisfying each individual investing pattern preferences.

In this study a model of a 20-year investment is developed comparing long-term returns of three asset classes: four housing markets, the stock market and government bonds. A comprehensive cost / benefit analysis is presented based on actual house, stock and bond valuations. Nominal periodic returns in the form of rents and dividends are juxtaposed with one-time acquisition costs like property transfer taxes and broker fees as well as periodical cost factors for maintenance, property taxation, or depot fees for stocks and bonds. Consumer price indices were taken into account to adjust for inflation to estimate real returns. Individual taxation is excluded as long as being dependent on the investor's residence.

Each of the four heterogeneous property markets is individually analyzed for strength and weakness as well its susceptibility to adverse events. Volatility of relevant input parameters such as fluctuations in rents or tax increases are discussed, and their impact on long-term return is shown. In addition, intra- and inter-correlations of the four housing market returns and for all asset classes studied, respectively, are provided. Risks of international real estate investments are assessed in order to provide strategies for minimization.

This study aims to provide insight and practical advice on how to address the Western real estate market, in particular of single-family homes, to generate adequate, predictable and steady return.

I.1 Types of Investments

Today's investment opportunities range on a spectrum from traditional to alternative asset classes in which can be invested privately or publicly on both the equity and debt side. A rough categorization may lead into a handful of classes of long-term assets:

a) Gold or other safe heavens in the real or crypto world
b) Government or corporate bonds
c) Real estate
d) Stocks
e) Collectibles
f) Soft assets like education, R&D knowledge, patents, reputation

Gold is one of the oldest forms of investments and one of the safest showing less risk compared to bonds and stocks (Yunus, 2020, p. 166; Sa-Aadu, 2010; Shobha, 2017; Baur, 2010, p. 228). The 10-year average annual demand is 4100 tons (2016) equaling a worth of EUR 217 bn as of November 2020 (ARD, 2020). Gold is used for jewelry (54%), investment (39%), technology (10%) and for central bank reserves (10%). It is easily tradeable in liquid forms of gold bars, massive gold coins like Krugerrand or exchange traded funds (ETFs) (Justetf, 2020). As for reasons of natural science gold bares no interest.

Other commodities sectors like oil, copper, or platinum. Moreover, crypto currencies can be considered.

Bonds (US SEC, 2020) are debt security like IOUs ("I owe you") which investors (lenders) may buy from governments (e.g., German "Bunds", U.S. "Treasuries" or "Munis") or corporations. The return of this investment is interest "coupons" as a specified rate during the life of the bond. After expiration the principal (face value) has to be repaid. The total return is determined by the market both when issuing a bond and when it is traded subsequently. In the event of a bankruptcy, bonds as first claim are preferred to stocks, thus being considered safer than the latter. The higher the risk the higher the risk premium, and thus, the return demanded by the investor. Credit ratings of the issuing entity help to determine riskiness of a bond. Bonds are closely linked to inflation and thus susceptible to inflation. Receiving a fixed coupon higher than inflation rates can depress returns unless the bonds are inflation-linked (ILBs). During the 2010s inflation was suppressed, and therefore, yields of German 10-year bonds even turned negative (ARD, 2020). Furthermore, liquidity risk applies to bonds from smaller issuing entities.

Stocks (US SEC, 2020) offer investors the greatest potential for growth over the long haul. Stock prices are highly volatile, and it may well be that an allocation in a particular single stock results in a negative long-term return. In the case of a bankruptcy, bonds are been paid out first, followed by *preferred* stockholders, whereas *common* stockholders are the last to receive any leftovers. A variety of funds (index funds, actively managed funds) are available to diversify over a large number of stocks at cost and the issuer risk. An investment in stocks and bonds can be intertwined by defining a percentage range (e.g., 45 – 55%) when excess valuations in one world leads to re-allocation of the assets to the other.

Often overlooked (J. Sa-Aadu, 2010, p. 533), investments in **real estate** are long-term, predictable and inflation-safe ("The state cannot print land.") but also inflexible and locally bound. Capital can be allocated directly in properties of various types such as office buildings, shopping centers or hotels in the commercial real estate market or in residential houses and apartments. Alternatively, numerous real estate funds or Real Estate Investment Trusts (REITs) have been established for investment.

Excurse 1: REITs

Real Estate Investment Trusts (REITs) were created Sept. 14, 1960 REITs by U.S. President Eisenhower (Semer, 2009, reit.com, 2012) signing the REIT Act title. The purpose was to "allow individual investors to invest in large-scale, income-producing real estate without actually having to actively buy commercial real estate (SEC, 2011). In June 1965 Continental Mortgage Investors became the first listed REIT on the New York Stock Exchange NYSE.

Being a commercial entity, a REIT buys, owns and operates real estate or real estate related assets which generate income by renting these houses, apartments, shopping malls, hotels, office buildings, commercial facilities and warehouses, hospitals, or just mortgages or loans. REITs also manage the real estate which distinguishes itself from house builders like Lennar Corp or Toll Brothers which build and acquire for reselling purposes. There are specialized REITs for each specific category.

A REIT is required to have 75% of its assets and derive 95% of its income connected to real estate investment. Greater than 90 percent of its taxable income has to be distributed to shareholders in the form of annual dividends (SEC, 2011). Typically, as much as 100% of its income is forwarded resulting not being liable to any tax payments at the corporate level. However, property related taxes still apply. There are further requirements as listed by the IRS (not all shown) (SEC, 2011):

• "Be managed by a board of directors or trustees,
• Have shares that are fully transferable,
• Have a minimum of 100 shareholders after its first year as a REIT,
• Have no more than 50 percent of its shares held by five or fewer individuals during the last half of the taxable year."

There are three categories of REITs: equity, mortgage, and hybrid (SEC, 2011). Equity REITs are the common class of REITs buying and renting real estate. In contrast, mortgage REITs act on the mortgage level by providing loans, and thus, invest indirectly in the real estate market. In this category leverage may increase return but also risk. By investing in debt securities secured by residential and commercial *mortgage, Hybrid REITs are a mixture of these two strate-gies.*

REITs can be open to the general public – "Publicly Traded REITs" or closed – "Non-Traded REITs". Despite that its shares are not traded on public stock exchanges like the NYSE these latter REITs can be acquired outside the public market at higher costs of 9-10 being similar of these buying "real" real estate as demonstrated in this study. Non-traded REITs therefore are more illiquid investments. Publicly Traded REITs in the contrary can be readily bought on the popular stock market at relatively low standard brokerage costs. Both types of REITs are regulated by the SEC and required to file regular disclosures.

A U.S.-REIT has to be managed on twofold (Ambrose, 2001): First, at an advisory level similar to mutual fund portfolio managers, who search for, evaluate, select and finally buy real estate assets. Second, these acquired assets have to be properly run by designated "property managers". These often-competing advisers vs. property management structures lead to an "outsourcing" of activities dividing REITs into inter-nally and externally advised entities. This was approved in 1986 by the U.S. Internal Revenue Service (IRS) referring them to having obtained 'self-advised' and 'self-managed' status.

Collectibles such as vintage cars or artworks are another class of long-term investments for experienced investors, who like to combine hobby and excitement with financial success.

"Invest in oneself" or so-called **soft assets** is a hard to grasp field still not being allowed to overlook. Enormous amounts of U.S. student loans (Report on the Economic Well-Being of U.S. Households in 2018, 2019) are an example of how to invest in soft assets. Other forms of soft assets are copyrights, patents or reputation in general which pay off in royalties. These investments often are not easily transferable.

I.2 Review of Relevant Literature

Ross et al. (1991) investigate real estate portfolio returns and risks from 1978 through 1985. Returns range from 10 % to 25 % and estimated risks sit in the 9 to 13 %

range midway between that of stocks and bonds. It has to be noted, though that this study reflects a high-inflationary environment with inflation figures in the 7 % range.

Sing et al. (2013) compare stocks and real estate as two important asset classes in an investors' portfolio. Correlating returns of stock market indices and total return National Council of Real Estate Investment Fiduciaries (NCREIF) subindices for the USA, the UK, Australia, Ireland, Singapore (IPD rental index) and Hong Kong (price index) of 1977-2008 reveals significant time-varying effects in the conditional covariance between stocks and real estate, except for Ireland and parts of the Australia, Hong Kong and Singapore markets. Diversification strategies (e.g., by using derivatives) need to be responsive to changing conditional correlations between the two asset classes to be effective when systematic shocks occur. Professional portfolio investors who determine weights solely based on a constant correlation assumption thus may see suboptimal returns.

Jadevicius (2019) discusses optimal Sharp ratios for 231 portfolios of non-listed real estate vehicles - Global Real Estate Fund Index (GREFI) in Asia Pacific, Europe and the United States. U.S. returns are at 2.7 % per quarter (annualized 11.2 % to compare with this study) higher than its European counterpart at 1.5 % per quarter (annualized 6.1 %) with a volatility of 1.1 % to 0.8 %, respectively. A pure Asia Pacific strategy would offer USA comparable returns with the lowest volatility. The optimal portfolio (the highest Sharpe ratio) results in an allocation of 40 % Asia Pacific and 30 % each U.S. and Europe generating quarterly returns of 2.3 % (annualized 9.5 %) at a volatility of 0.5 %.

Oertel et al. (2019) analyze whether European real estate investors should diversify into the U.S. market. In contrast to our study, Oertel focuses on 12 real estate sectors, wherefrom 11 are commercial real estate. U.S. apartments being the only non-commercial property sector, which shows the highest 11.6% return at medium risk level. Thereby, two hypotheses are confirmed: Investments in U.S. properties improve the risk-return profile for European real estate investors. However, potentials for the geographical diversification decrease due to increasing global market integration.

Dynamics of the European housing market were assessed by Begatti et al. (2018). Comparing housing data of 47 cities across eight European markets from 2000 to 2017 uitlizing fundamental explanatory variables as in Case and Shiller (2003). Notable correlations were found: Change in employment is not statistically significant in six out of the eight markets, the regressor of change in population is significantly, positively correlated with house prices in contrast to Case and Shiller, who also find negative correlations. Furthermore, the relationship between the mortgage rate and housing returns is negative, which was never statistically significant in the analysis provided by Case and Shiller. Remarkably, Spain shows a deviating behavior.

Faguzza et al. (2007) examine portfolio choices for a long-term investment horizon (up to 10 years) of a risk-adverse investor who diversifies among European stocks, bonds, real estate, and cash. Their calculations reveal that an allocation between 12% and 44% in real estate are considered to be optimal and that its portfolio share increases the longer the investment horizon. All investment classes (stocks, bonds, and real estate) do not appear excessively risky in the long-term, "so that the demand for cash is rather limited or even absent. Real estate performance is negatively related to the lagged short-term real interest rate and to past inflation" (p. 73). Therefore, while being a poor instrument to cover inflation risk in the short run, real estate appears to be the best long-term inflation hedge.

Older data from 1953 – 1971 compiled by Farmer et al. (1977, p. 115) shows that "U.S. government bonds and bills were a complete hedge against expected inflation, and private residential real estate was a complete hedge against both expected and unexpected inflation. In contrast, stock returns were not only negatively correlated to the expected component of the inflation rate but probably also to the unexpected component".

Antonakaki et al. (2017) demonstrate the significantly negative correlations between stock prices and inflation in the United States over the period of 1791–2015. Significantly positive correlations were observed in the 1840s, 1860s, 1930s, and in 2011. However, inflationary shocks have little long-term impact on real stock returns. Lee et al. (2014) show similar results for Europe.

Ibbotson (2010) questions the impact of the long-term (passive) asset allocation policy of a mixed portfolio relative to the impact of active performance derived from market timing, security selection, and fees. He finds the average peer group performance makes up about three-quarters of the variation in time-series returns. Therefore, returns come from general market movement rather than asset allocation within the group.

Hui et al. (2016) investigate the cointegration relationship among nine securitized real estate indices, which are divided into three groups: North America, Europe and Asia. Hui et al. show that all three regional markets follow a similar pattern of cointegration: a gradually increasing common trend before the global financial crisis in 2007, reaching a peak during the crisis, and dying down gradually thereafter. Cointegration in North America precedes Asian and European countries, "showing that North America is the source of cointegration, while Asia and Europe are the recipients" (p. 1).

In a more recent study, Abuzayed et al. (2020) evaluate the role of real estate in stock portfolios in three major European countries (Germany, the UK, and France) from 2003 to 2018 including crisis environments. They show that in stressed periods REITs provide less diversification potential of stock portfolios.

Sa-Aadu et al. (2010) make a case of inclusion of real estate in diversified U.S.-based investor portfolios over the period from 1972–2008. An optimal tangency portfolio in good times consist of 25% each of small-cap and international stocks, 22% government bonds, 15% REITs and 9% medium- and large-cap stocks. In economic downturns, the proportion of government bonds doubles (53%) and precious metals (28%) as well as REITs (19%) raise. Only equity REITs, precious metals commodities and government bonds have a nonzero tangency portfolio allocation in both states of the economy, and thus, being key asset classes in a hedging strategy.

Hedging by U.S. real estate assets also is studied by Christou et al. (2018) against non-housing CPI for the period of 1953-2016. While they find correlations in the short term, they fail to show evidence of a long-run relationship, most likely indicating existing bubbles. Still, housing seems to act as a positive over-hedge for inflation.

Yunus (2020) study linkages among gold, stocks, bonds and real estate for the years 1985-2017. Similar to the results presented in this study, a positive correlation between 0.431 and 0.496 for real estate and the stock market, and a negative connection of −0.136 to −0.150 between real estate and bonds are found. In contrast, gold being long-term integrated with stocks, bonds, and real estate cannot be used as a hedge for long-term investment horizons. However, it fulfills its function as a save haven in crisis periods.

Yang et. al. (2012) study daily index returns of the S&P 500 from 1999 to 2008, U.S. corporate bonds, and their real estate counterparts (REITs and CMBS). "REIT and stock returns show asymmetries in their conditional correlation, suggesting reduced hedging potential of REITs in volatile times like the significant structural break in correlations caused by the financial crisis of 2008" (p. 491). Pairwise conditional correlations between these asset classes reveal that four pairs, stock-corporate bonds, CMBS-stock, equity REIT-corporate bonds, and equity REIT-CMBS, are a good hedge to each other.

Richter et al. (2011) look at real estate return distributions for German commercial and residential properties. Building characteristics seem to have less impact than the differentiation between capital growth and income

17

return latter being not abruptly changing continuous cash flows.

Guidolin et al. (2020) examine the predictability of excess real-world returns for both private and public real estate including transaction costs for a range of investment horizons years using different models. Data collected from 1978-2018 for up to 5-year investments show high accuracy in prediction of real estate excess performance.

II. SCOPE

As people appear to think more and more short-term – the U.S. savings rate declined from well over 10% in the 1960s (Fed S. L., 2020) to about 7% recently, this thesis aims to provide a different view of long-term investing into residential properties. Europe and the U.S. as large and open markets were selected as prime examples for studying total returns at housing markets over a 20-year long-term investment.

Most people refer to gold, bonds and stocks when thinking about investing. A house often is considered as "being" a place to live rather than "having" an investment (Waymond Rodgers, 2017). Being a homeowner encourages the feeling of being safe and shielded from the dangerous world out there just beginning of the front door. A value-based thinking seems not to be the first priority. The same applies to other forms like shops, offices or infrastructure real estate assets. Hardly anyone is aware of the rent being paid by the coffee-shop when staring his or her day with a delicious café latte. To the extreme, on New York's Fifth Avenue in the 50s-blocks (Chainstoreage, 2020), tenants like Tiffany's, Bergdorf Goodman or Louis Vuitton pay an average of USD 3,000 per sq. ft. unless righteously owning their properties like the Morton F. Plant House by Cartier (Dunlap, 2000).

This work focuses on the single-family home market and its long-term returns. Usually, the only time when home valuations and financing costs come into a normal person's mind is when buying their own house and applying for a mortgage. The investor in mind, however, needs to be more affluent as this research aims to investigate investments in single-family homes as a whole. Other forms of applying capital to the real estate market (e.g., REITs) exist for smaller wallets similar of those of the stock market.

This comprehensive study targets to include most relevant aspects of real estate investing and is not limited to an investor's domicile hence individual taxation is excluded where individual strategies need to be developed and applied (Jeffers, 2007; Goddard, 2012).

Average and total returns of an exemplary 20-year investment in the four housing markets plus the stock and bond markets for comparison are given as well as the obstacles and risks of each are discussed. Based on these results, risk minimizing strategies are derived and a concluding recommendation is provided.

Limitations are that future considerations are solely based on trends which are derived from past data from 20 up to 44 years. Though modeled, actual changes in taxes, law and developments of the financial market cannot be foreseen. The four regions are exemplary for the main markets in Europe and the United States. Specific and local abnormalities may apply and are not subject to this study.

III. SELECTION AND OVERVIEW OF THE HOUSING MARKETS

In contrast to the stock market, investing in real estate is considered as being a safe, maybe even slightly boring bet influenced by behavioral biases (Pandey, 2019). Excluding the not readily accessible commercial real estate market for individual investors, this study focusses on single-family homes. In this real-world example, an imaginary investor is guided in his process to make fact-based choices on the capital allocation among these markets. Staying focused two regions on each side of the Atlantic are analyzed (see Table 1). Selection criteria were derived from the scope to present representative and accessible markets which reflect the characteristics of its area whilst not being too specific in terms of cultural, financial or historical peculiarities. The following criteria of how to select these four markets were set up:

- Having a population of > 3 M,
- Being representative for its continent,
- Be part of a larger U.S. state or being a large country in Europe,

- Lack abnormalities (e.g., extreme volatility in Florida, out-of-average property taxes in New Jersey, Swiss investment restrictions or being incoherent like Italy),
- Be distinct from the other side of the Atlantic (thus excluding, e.g., the UK),
- Being locally distant,
- Having data available for ≥ 20 years.

III.1 United States

Starting in the western hemisphere well-known California as the most populous U.S. state with more than 39.8 million residents, and the second most popular destination for foreign homebuyers, next to Florida was a natural choice (Globalpropertyguide, 2020), accounting for about 12% of all international purchases in the U.S. every year. As being both a business as well as a tourist destination, California is highly attractive to foreign buyers. About one-third of foreign purchases in California were made by Chinese citizens, followed by UK buyers (20%), and Indian and Mexican citizens (10% each, Globalpropertyguide, 2020).

III. Selection and Overview of the Housing Markets

Southern California in particular had been popular with Chinese accounting for about one-third of foreign purchases in California, followed by UK citizens, Mexicans and Indian buyers at 20%, 10%, and 10%, respectively (Globalpropertyguide, 2020).

Narrowing further down the well-documented metro area, *San Diego* was chosen as – while not being a hub city like San Francisco – still is a thriving region and a desirable place to live. Being close to Los Angeles, the area is accessible from within the U.S. as well as the whole world. Selected direct flights to San Diego Airport are available from Europe. San Diego was preferred above San Francisco and Los Angeles for its ability to balance out the main focus of foreign investors towards big cities with the broader and more representative view towards California as a whole. Alternatively, Sacramento as an example of a rural but large city or Santa Barbara with its mixture of wealth and remoteness could have been used for this study.

Being another favorite destination for international investors, the East to Center U.S. the "Lone Star State" Texas was chosen. 9% to 12% of all U.S. homes sold to foreign buyers (Globalpropertyguide, 2020) wherein like in California Mexicans are a major home buying group as well as buyers from India (13%). Being somewhat less international fewer Chinese (3%), UK citizens (4%), and Canadians (3%) are seen as buyers. In contrast to investors from abroad, Texas is being popular amongst for domestic buyers because of – similar to Florida – it does not have state income tax.

Texas is a growing state which lacked much of the impact from the 2007-2009 housing bubble. In the 1980s (Financial Times, 2016) an oil-price related bubble burst and shielded this market from the bubble of this century. As a large metro area **Dallas** can represent an alternative to San Diego better than Florida or the very distinct – albeit attractive – market of New York City. Dallas/Fort Worth airport is one of the main hubs in the U.S. and destination of numerous worldwide nonstops.

Despite its size and population, the alternatives are limited. From an investor's perspective only Houston and the San Antonio / Austin area seem attractive unless other business or personal connections exist.

III.2 Europe

In good-old Europe not many large markets exist. From the Netherlands (or more broadly the BeNeLux area), France, the UK, Italy, *Spain* and *Germany* the latter two were selected. Italy appeared to be fragmented between the rich North and the poor South, the UK is juridical in between the U.S. and Europe, whereas France and the Netherlands were considered as being not locally distant enough. In addition, France in particular splits up in Paris and the rest. This centrism is less seen in Spain (Eurostat, Eurostat, 2020) and not at all in Germany. Both Spain (with Barcelona and Madrid) and Germany (with Frankfurt and Munich) boast with two major airport hubs, respectively. These two countries were selected as whole for lacking specific metro area data. Spain for example has a single-family housing market just 5 times larger than the San Diego metro area still having 14 times more inhabitants. In contrast to Germany, Spain as a Latin country provides another set of differentiation.

Table 1: Overview of Main Market Data

This table shows the main characteristics of the 4 house markets selected (Germany, Spain, San Diego metro, and Dallas metro) including demographic data and JLL transparency parameters, housing units and median values, and market size. Sources: Population (Eurostat and U.S. Census), JLL indices (Global Real Estate Transparency Index), Sales and total single-family homes Germany (Statista), Spanish housing stock (Statista), Spanish home sales (INE), San Diego and Dallas homes mean values and days on market (Zillow), San Diego sales (InfoSparks) and Dallas sales (Santarelli), San Diego and Dallas housing units (U.S. Department of Housing and Urban Development), Professionally managed market size estimates (MSCI)

	Germany	Spain	San Diego	Dallas
Population ('000)	83,019	46,935	3,383	7,573
Population grow y/y	0.27%	0.59%	1.00%	1.90%
JLL transparency tier / rank / index	high / 10 / 1.93	transparent / 19 / 2.16	high / 2 / 1.35	
Housing Units (M)	15.9	25.7	1.2	1.0
Median Value (9/2020)			668,138	272,699
Owner occupied	45%	79%	57%	64%
Single Family homes on market (9/2020)			7,835	30,906
Median days to pending (9/2020)			8	23
Sales of dwellings p.a.	276,300	419,931	32,434	2,928
Market size in b USD (2019)	580	111	22	10

III.3 Benchmarking Assets: Stocks and Bonds

To classify overall returns of the single-family real estate market both the stock and the bond markets are used as a well-known and highly liquid references for comparison. This study refrains from analyzing bonds and equities per se. Therefore, broad worldwide indexes for stocks (MSCI world, MXWO) and government bonds (FTSE World Government Bond Index WGBI) are used to represent the stock and bond markets as a whole.

IV. DATA AND METHODOLOGY

IV.1 Calculation of Base Returns

Base returns are the average annual returns of the time-dependent valuation of each asset measured at the index level before any costs such as, e.g., property taxes and before any yield like rents or dividends.

IV.1.1 Real Estate Data

To compare base returns of single-family real estate in the four countries of this study housing price indices for Germany, Spain, and the San Diego and Dallas metro areas were utilized.

Two sets of annual German housing data of all dwellings since 1975 (VDP, 2020) were aligned in year 2017 as the longest running set stopped being provided thenceforth (see Figure 1). Quarterly indices of all dwellings for Spain (ISI Emerging Markets Group, 2020) were obtained where each Q4 value was extracted (see Figure 2). Prior to 2007, figures

31

were only available based on square footage. Hence, these numbers were equalized towards the house price index that year and calculated back to 1987.

Figure 1: Wohnimmobilienpreisindex (Residential property price index) Deutsche Bundesbank

This figure shows the German House Price Index measuring all types of dwellings in the whole country. The index of 2010 (data available until 2017) was merged with the index of 2016 and normalized to 1999=100. Dating back to 1975 the steady rise came to a halt in 1995 plateauing until 2010 followed by a rapid rise (source: BIS).

Figure 2: Spanish Property Price Index

This figure shows the quarterly government data for Spanish housing market derived as price per square foot from 1995 (December values) to 2019 consisting of all dwellings. After 2007 prices per unit were compiled by the National Statistic Office. The 1995 to 2006 prices per square foot were converted to prices per unit. All data was normalized to 1999 = 100. Spain was the center of the European house price bubble which inflates in the years prior to 2007 followed by a decline thereafter. As of 2019 the house prices have not fully recovered to their peak level (source: BIS).

For the United States the broadly used S&P/Case-Shiller indices were derived from the Federal Reserve Bank of St. Louis. The monthly San Diego metro Case Shiller index SDXR (Shiller, Yahoo finance,

2020) is available back to 1987 (see Figure 3). The index is calculated with and without seasonal adjustments. For comparison with the European data each December value was carried over thus eliminating seasonal adjustments. To compensate for traditionally slower sales volume in wintertime the adjusted values were used. The corresponding TX-Dallas Home Price Index (Shiller, Yahoo finance, 2020) started to be compiled in 1999 limiting the data set to 20 years (Figure 4). All data was normalized towards the year 1999 = 100.

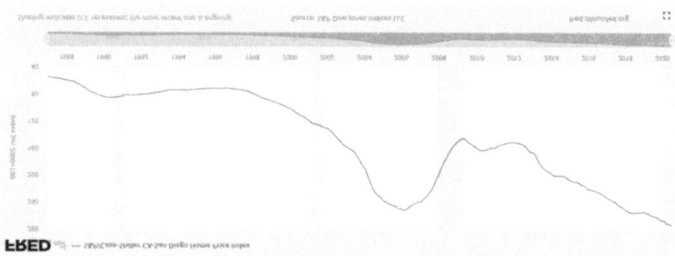

Figure 3: San Diego House Prices

Case Shiller San Diego Home Price Index (SDXR), St. Lois Fed; January 2000 = 100 (Fed S. L., St. Louis Fed, 2020)

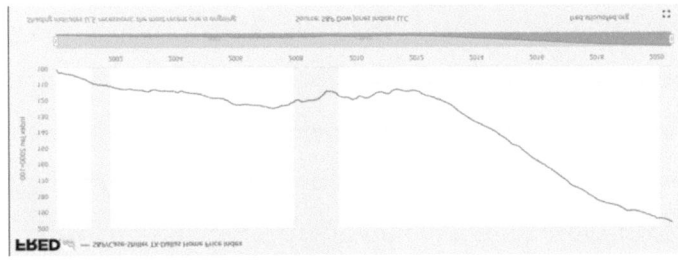

Figure 4: Dallas House Prices

Case Shiller Dallas Home Price Index (DAXR), St. Loius Fed; January 2000 = 100 (Shiller, Yahoo Finance, 2020)

IV.1.2 Stocks and Bonds

The MSCI World Index (MSCI, 2020), "MSCI world", comprises of 1607 large and mid-cap listed companies across 23 developed markets. It "covers approximately 85% of the free float-adjusted market capitalization in each country" (MSCI, 2020). Representing a broad cross-section, it is used as a common global or world benchmark. As of current roughly two thirds of its value represents the U.S. As a result of the run-up of tech stock Apple, Microsoft, Facebook, Amazon and Alphabet represent a 14% share. To compare the MSCI World Index to the housing market indices, its price component was used, and

35

the dividends were derived separately from Bloomberg. To compensate for the Dot-com bubble the 1999 index value can be exponentially regressed towards the 1995-2005 period to a 1999 starting MSCI world index value of 1076 resulting in an annual base return of 4% (not shown in table). A more realistic approach is provided (and further explained in the discussion) by investing 20% each of the total capital available over a period of consecutive 5 years. The remained amount may be held at a bank account for which the mean annual inflation rate of 1999-2004 of 2.49% was calculated and used. This approach results in a higher base return of 4.70%. Normalization was carried out towards the year 1999 = 100.

As a broad government-based bond index, the FTSE World Government Bond Index (WGBI, "FTSE bonds"), was selected being a broad benchmark for the global sovereign fixed income market. It includes fixed-rate, local currency denominated investment-grade sovereign debt from over 20 countries with minimum maturities of at least one year. Coupons are reinvested hence all returns are included in the performance index. Again, data was normalized towards the year 1999 = 100.

All collected and normalized data – excluding all costs, returns and taxes – was aligned and plotted to provide an overview of the base indexes (see Figure 5). All rows of data are available from the year 1999. The 2000 Dot-Com bubble in stocks and the 2006 housing bubble in the housing markets of San Diego and Spain can be readily seen, whereas Germany and Dallas remained unaffected. It is emphasized that normalization of raw data occurred at the height of the stock bubble demonstrating the need for special consideration as discussed.

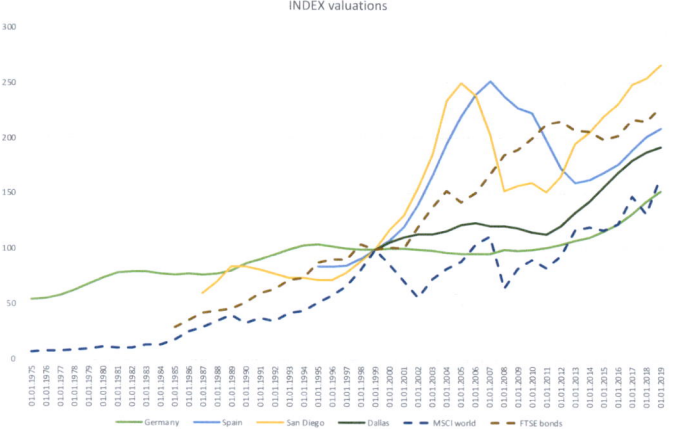

Figure 5: House Price Indices, Stock and Bond Market Indices

This figure shows the normalized raw house price indices for the four areas covered (Germany, Spain, San Diego metro, and Dallas metro), as well as the MSCI world stocks and FTSE world government bonds. All data represent the raw index values from the start of each data set derived and normalized for 1999 = 100. Index values exclude costs, returns and taxes except for bonds having its coupons included. The 2007 housing bubble can be seen in the housing markets of Spain and Dallas as well as the Dot-Com bubble in stocks peaking in 1999. This figure illustrates the need of smoothing the stock investment over a period of 5 years in particular as this 20-year study covers the years 1999-2019 (source: BIS, Bloomberg).

IV.1.3 Method for Base Return Calculation

The timeline of the data reaches back at least 20 years. To analyze the data, valuations at the beginning and at the end were obtained to calculate trends. To compensate for abnormalities other figures or calculations were used and described accordingly. The n = 20-year average base return from x = 1999 to 2019 was calculated using the exponential / compound interest method:

$$base\ return_n = \sqrt[n]{\Delta index_{x+n,x}} - 1$$

$$base\ return_{20} = \sqrt[20]{(index_{2019} - index_{1999})} - 1$$

Standard deviations and Sharpe ratios were derived subsequently. All values were calculated on the whole investment for all 20 years, even for the 5-year investment strategy, where the return was calculated and added for each series of stock purchases.

IV.2 Costs, Inflation and Rents

Starting from the base return relevant costs and proceedings were subsequently included in the calculation. Figures for investment related costs, the inflation, and the rental income was derived from various sources cited hereto.

IV.2.1 Transaction Costs and Taxes - Germany

Costs on buying real estate arise on various levels (Globalpropertyguide, 2020).

Germany		
Real estate transfer tax	3.50 % - 6.50 %	buyer
Notary fees	1.20 % - 1.50 %	buyer
Registration fees	0.80 % - 1.20 %	buyer
Broker's fee seller	1.5 % - 3 % (+ 19 % VAT)	buyer
Broker's fee buyer	1.5 % - 3 % (+ 19 % VAT)	seller
Buyer's costs	7.23 % - 12.77 %	
Seller's costs	1.79 % - 3.57 %	
Roundtrip transaction costs	9.02 % - 16.34 %	
Roundtrip transaction costs (mean)	12.7 %	

Real property transfer tax ("Grunderwerbssteuer)" varies depending on respective federal state and are for 2020 (Germany Trade & Invest, 2020):

„3.5% Bavaria, Saxony
4.5% Hamburg

5.0% Baden-Württemberg, Bremen, Mecklenburg-Vorpommern, Niedersachsen, Rheinland-Pfalz, Saxony-Anhalt

6.0% Berlin, Hessen

6.5% Brandenburg, North Rhine-Westphalia, Saarland, Schleswig-Holstein, Thuringia"

All other fees are for a typical house. On higher transfer values broker fees can be negotiated.

As common in German culture, property tax (in German "Grundsteuer") has to be calculated in a complicated manner (Bundesfinanzministerium, 2019). There are three components which the product is calculated according to the formula: "Wert" x "Steuermesszahl" x "Hebesatz". "Wert" which is the assessed value is calculated itself being based on the value of the lot "Bodenrichtwert" and the rental value "Nettokaltmiete". Latter is dependent where the property is located. Further, the age, type of real estate and the lot size are relevant. The "Steuermesszahl" depends on the appreciation calculated from base values since 1935 or 1964, respectively. For certain entities in order to make renting affordable, this value is reduced by 25%. Lastly, the

"Hebesatz" is a factor set by the local government and varies widely (see Figure 6).

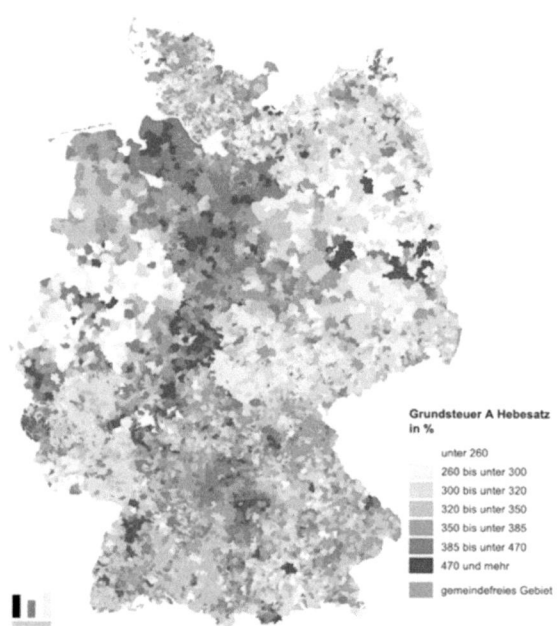

Figure 6: German Property Tax Lifting Rate

German "Hebesätze" (Bundesamt, 2019) In German municipal tax law, the Hebesatz (lifting rate) is a factor which the tax base is multiplied with to determine the tax liability. This figure shows the local variations of the lifting factor applied.

12 municipalities do not collect property tax at all (Sueddeutsche Zeitung, 2018). The mean German

property tax (Dasinvestment, 2020) (Bundesfinanzministerium, Vergleich.de, 2019) is calculated as a mean of 0.14%. Unlike in other countries, it is common for Germany to pass the property tax on towards the tenant. In this study, it is taken fully into account therefore offering additional income of 2 to 3 % after n = 20 years when renting out the investment property.

$$additional\ return_n = (1 + property\ tax\ rate)^n - 1$$

$$additional\ return_{20} = (1 + 0.0014)^{20} - 1 = 2.8\ \%$$

IV.2.2 Transaction Costs and Taxes - Spain

The Spanish acquisition costs can be summarized as follows (Globalpropertyguide, 2020):

Spain		
Property transfer tax	6 % - 10 %	buyer
Notary fee	0.03 % - 0.45 %	buyer
Registration fee	0.02 % -18 %	buyer
Broker's fee seller	2.50 % - 3 %	seller
Buyer's costs	6.05 % - 10.63 %	
Seller's costs	2.50 % - 3.00 %	
Roundtrip transaction costs	8.55 % - 13.63 %	
Roundtrip transaction costs (mean)	11.1 %	

Spanish property taxes are twofold. First, the annual real estate related tax Impuesto sobre Bienes Inmuebles (IBI) (Impuestos, 2020) is due at a rate of 0.3 percent to 1.1 percent of the property's cadastral valuation. Exact valuations were not accessible, nor could a mean value be obtained. One given example (Myspanishresidency, 2020) states a flat of 350.000 EUR with a corresponding IBI between 500 EUR and 700 EUR per year equaling 0.17%.

Second, a Spanish wealth tax exists which is being levied on the personal possession including real estate. This tax also applies to foreign real estate investors. Its maximum value of 3.03% from 10.7 M EUR onwards (2016) is a significant drag on any returns (Andalucia-Lawyers, 2016). In the study 1 M EUR would imply a tax rate of roughly 1%. An exemption of 700,000 EUR on the tax base is granted. As the scope of this study is a long-term investment the implications of compound interest have to be addressed. Assessed values will likely increase significantly faster than inflation and it may be well assumed that the tax rates will rise – if at all – at an inflation-based rate thus reducing the tax exemption and drive the effective tax rate higher. As a major drag, this tax levied on the personal side cannot be neglected in this study, hence a 0.75% figure was added. Variations hereto can be estimated as discussed in the volatility section of this study.

IV.2.3 Transaction Costs and Taxes - United States

Transaction Costs in the United States (Globalpropertyguide, 2020) are as follows:

United States		
Title search and insurance	0.5 % - 1.0 %	buyer
Recording fee	0.20 % - 0.50 %	buyer
Seller's legal fees	0.5 % - 1.0 %	seller
Buyer's legal fees	0.5 % - 1.0 %	buyer
Real property transfer tax	1 % - 1.425 %	seller
Real estate broker's fee	6.00 %	seller
Buyer's costs	1.20 % - 2.50 %	
Seller's costs	7.50 % - 8.425 %	
Roundtrip transaction costs	8.70 % - 10.925 %	
Roundtrip transaction costs (mean)	9.81 %	

It has to be noted that a portion of the broker fees - albeit at 6% similar to Germany's - can be used to negotiate a discount when purchasing the property.

California property taxes are limited to 1% of the assessed value plus bonds approved by the local public. To reflect that matter, a 1.1% property tax was selected for this study. Proposition 13 (Equalization, 2019) limits the property tax in California, whereas proposition 8 (Equalization, 2020) allows for a temporary decline in value. To reflect that the 1.1% of property tax is levied upon a 2% increase on the purchase price of 1999 and calculated as a percentage in 2009. To compensate for the housing crisis the 2009 value was exponentially regressed towards 2007-2012. Proposition 13 thus reduces the effective property tax rate from 1.1% to 0.8% over the course of a 20-year investment.

Excurse 2: Proposition 13 – California

In the 1970s (Vranjes, 2020) *residents got increasingly frustrated with high inflation and soaring property taxes. Being part of a nationwide anti-tax wave, in 1978 California voters approved proposition 13* (Equalization, 2019) *which limits the property tax rate to 1 percent plus the rate necessary to fund local voter-approved, rolled back the assessed values back to 1975 and limits the annual increase to 2% unless the property is sold or altered (e.g., new construction).*

"Section 1. (a) The maximum amount of any ad valorem tax on real property shall not exceed one percent (1%) of the full cash value of such property. The one percent (1%) tax to be collected by the counties and apportioned according to law to the districts within the counties."

— California Constitution Article XIII A

After passing, property-tax revenues plummeted nearly 60 percent (Haberman, 2016). The following years the share of property taxes declined as a share of government revenue. The shortfall was filled by increases in utility taxes as on hotels and sales. Especially, in wealthy areas it is not uncommon for young family just moving in to see a much higher tax bill than an older couple's next door in a nearly identical house.

To illustrate the consequences of proposition 13 a typical bay area single-family house is shown. 1105 Hidden Oaks Dr, Menlo Park, CA 94025 (Zillow, 2020) was purchased before proposition 13 took place. During the years the assessed value increased to USD 186,127 in 2018 resulting in a tax bill of USD 3,219 that year - it should be that there are additions to the bill unrelated to the assessed value thus resulting in a proportionally higher tax.

The house was sold on September 4th, 2019 for USD 3,200,000. The property tax for 2020 therefore will increase to about USD 35,200; more than tenfold.

Proposition 13 helped older people to stay in their home but caused a serious financial crisis at the local government level. They had to lay off employees and cut costs but also forced them to become more efficient. Since 1978, Californians have become accustomed and happy about proposition 13 which became deep-rooted in their minds.

From an investors perspective the short-term effect is marginal, however, it becomes significant in the long run, especially in years of high inflation. Thus, proposition 13 is a major factor when putting money into U.S. real estate.

Texas levies property taxes on several levels. Combined property tax rates in the Dallas metro area are 1.992% (Smartasset, 2020).

IV.2.4 Transaction Costs and Taxes – Stocks and Bonds

For funds a 2% management fee and a 20% cut of profits was the industry's standard for years. Due to the rise of exchange traded funds, rising competition and low-cost brokers, management, transaction, bank, and depot fees have been under pressure for some time. Especially, for index funds costs have come down significantly. To cover all fees transaction costs have been set at 0.25% for each buying and selling transaction, analog to Guidolin et al. (2020).

Based on the current stock and bond prices the index itself excludes real-world management fees and is not accessible as an investment directly. A variety of ETFs linked to indices are available on the free market. Index fund fees and bank commissions herewith are set at 0.25% per year.

IV.3 Inflation, Maintenance, and Rents

The inflation rates for Germany DECPI2005 (Statistisches Bundesamt, 2020), Spain ESCPI2013

((INE), 2020), and the U.S. USCPI31011913 (U.S. Bureau of Labor Statistics, 2020) of the 20-year period were used for each of the three countries. The corresponding values for the stock and bond markets were calculated being the arithmetic mean of those.

Maintenance costs are calculated based on a replacement of 25% of the property value (half of 50% of the total property cost; the remainder being the parcel) over 30 years. For California a correction factor of 2/3 is allied to compensate for high land prices. For stocks and bonds a depot fee was taken into account to cover the expenses relate for handling and maintaining the stock bond portfolio.

German (Investment, 2019) (Globalpropertyguide, 2020) and Spanish (Spain, 2019) (Brainsre, 2020) (Globalpropertyguide, 2020) rental income yields are provided for the country as a whole, whereas rental values in the U.S. refer to San Diego county and the Dallas-Fort Worth area (Towncharts, 2020), respectively. During the extensive search similar multiple figures for Germany and Spain were derived. However, these did not differ significantly.

Mean values were used for calculation. Dividends were considered equivalent to the rental income of a real estate property investment and thus handled identically.

IV.4 Method for Real Return Calculation

Transaction costs including associated taxes were included both ways assuming a disposal of the investment after the n = 20-year period. Individual taxes were not taken into account for both the real estate and the stock and bond parts. Acquisition costs were spread out over the 20-year period of this study. The assembled costs were added towards as percentages to the base return according to the formula:

$$return\ real_n = base\ return_n - property\ taxes$$
$$- transaction\ costs/n - inflation_n$$

$$return\ after\ rents, dividends = return\ real$$
$$+ rents, dividends$$

In this study, an imaginary investment of legal funds is assumed. The investor may be based in Europe or the U.S. or even anywhere else hence no particular base currency was selected. USD or EUR may be exchanged at the current rate (FX). As the calculation is scalable a given amount in USD may be invested in the corresponding number of EUR which might be higher and lower. It is assumed that during the investment period all fluctuations in FX will level out. Any FX gain or loss will be in addition to the calculation presented.

As initial capital a 1 million of no particular currency in 1999 was given. Based on the return after rents or dividends its final value before taxes in 2019 was calculated.

A simple exponential formula (power function) for returns after n years is used:

$$ROI_n = capital\ invested$$
$$* \ [(1 + annual\ return\ real)^n - 1]$$

IV.5.1 Robustness Analysis

Returns and expenses are subject to fluctuations which were simulated for proceeds, property tax, maintenance costs (bank fees for stocks and bonds), and rents (or dividends). Disposal values were altered for a decrease of 2 standard deviations - equaling 95.45% probability - of the simulated sale value after 20 years and the reduced return rate exponentially decreased. The %-difference of the ROI after 20 years was calculated. Constant 10% hikes of property tax, maintenance costs and rents were derived. No property tax-like value for the MSCI world and FTSE bonds leave these values unchanged; its maintenance costs – depot and bank fees – however, were increased by 10%. Being a performance index, no increase in returns was calculated for FTSE bonds. Moreover - aside from the risk of default – coupons / returns are fixed.

IV.5.2 Shock Simulation

Besides catastrophes like environmental disasters or warfare, a longer-lasting economic shock like a downturn of the economy needs to be taken into consideration when investing in real estate. To investigate the resilience of the proposed model towards unforeseen events and thus of an investment in real estate a severe one-time shock event a 50% loss of returns over a period of 3 years was calculated by decreasing the rents and dividends. Having coupons at a fixed rate no alteration for bonds was assumed. Final percent change of 20-year ROI was derived in comparison to the non-shock model. It was further assumed that in the long-term the shock event does not alter the disposal value of the asset as they return to their path of pretended growth in the long run.

V. EMPIRICAL RESULTS

V.1 Return Performance

Returns were calculated based in the index returns for a 20-year investment horizon with compound interest (see Table 2). Acquisition costs were aliquoted; expenses and income were added as percentages. Maintenance fees cover bank-related expenses for stocks and bonds. For the FTSE world bond index as a performance index, there is no need to add a coupon return.

Adjusted for inflation, real estate returns before rental income of the four housing markets range from -0.92% for Germany to +1.05% for San Diego. The rental "dividend" turns the yearly compound, inflation-adjusted return positive for all markets to 2.04% to 4.75% comparing to 4.80% for stocks and 1.48% for bonds. Return on investment (ROI) therefore comes to 1.5 to 2.5 million on a 20-year investment of 1 million (not linked to any specific currency).

Table 2: Calculation of Returns

This table shows the return calculations for all available years. Returns were calculated exponentially beginning at the start of each index until 2019. For the 20-year period from 1999-2019 mean returns were calculated accordingly. A 5-year investment strategy of 20% allocation of stocks leaving the remainder in an inflation-linked account until fully invested was used for the MSCI world stock index to mimic a regularly used method and to correct for the 1999 Dot-com bubble. Costs (source: California State Board of Equalization, Globalpropertyguide, Smartasset) were subtracted accordingly; the acquisition costs of the investment were spread out over the 20-year period. Inflation (source: Statistisches Bundesamt, INE, U.S. Bureau of Labor Statistics) was deducted and rents and dividends added, respectively (source: Bloomberg, Das Investment, Globalpropertyguide, Central Bank of Spain, Brainsre, Towncharts). Total Return of Investment (ROI) of 1 million for 20 years was calculated using the real return including income. For all housing markets inflation-adjusted real return before income is negative except for San Diego. The corresponding figures for the stock and bond markets are positive, latter having the coupons included in its pre-income return. (opposite page)

		Germany	Spain	San Diego	Dallas	MSCI world	FTSE bonds
INDEX RETURN	Mean (all data)	2.39%	3.90%	4.80%	3.33%	7.43%	6.24%
	Mean (1999-2019)	2.15%	3.76%	5.02%	3.33%	4.70%	4.21%
	Standard deviation	0.030	0.089	0.117	0.039	0.183	0.065
	Sharp ratio	0.71	0.42	0.43	0.85	0.26	0.65
COSTS	Transaction (round trip)	12.7%	11.1%	9.8%	9.8%	0.50%	0.50%
	Property tax	0.15%	0.92%	0.78%	1.99%	0.00%	0.00%
	Maintainance	0.83%	0.83%	0.56%	0.83%	0.25%	0.25%
	Return after costs	0.53%	1.45%	3.19%	0.02%	4.42%	3.94%
INFLATION	Mean	1.45%	2.06%	2.14%	2.14%	1.95%	1.95%
	Real return	-0.92%	-0.61%	1.05%	-2.12%	2.47%	1.99%
INCOME	Rents / dividends	2.96%	4.48%	3.58%	6.88%	2.32%	0.00%
	Real return incl. income	2.04%	3.87%	4.63%	4.75%	4.80%	1.99%
ROI	Total 20 years (1999 = 1.00)	1.50	2.14	2.47	2.53	2.55	1.48
	Investment (m)	1.00	1.00	1.00	1.00	1.00	1.00

Monitoring the actual return over the course of the investment not-recoverable acquisition and disposal costs were rightly deducted in the first year setting back stock and bond funds by 0.5% and real estate investments by 9.8% to 12.7%. This lag is compensated by excess returns to inflation in 3 to 7 years Germany being the latest to pass. With the exception of Germany – which never exceeds the returns of FTSE bonds – all other three housing markets pass the index within 5 years (see Figure 7).

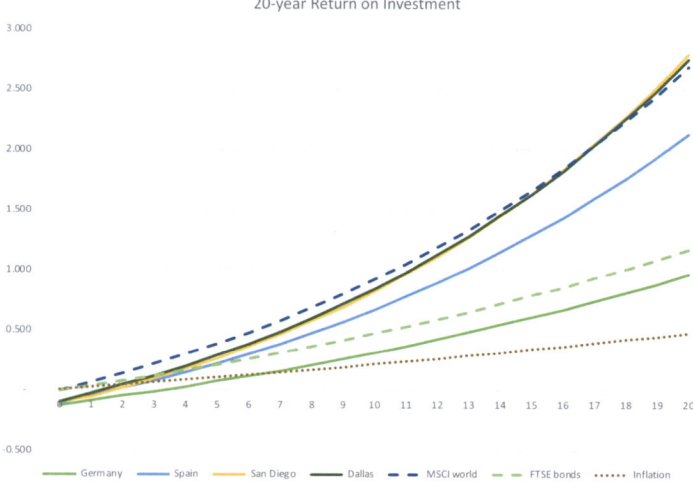

Figure 7: 20-year Return on Investment (ROI)

This figure shows the return of a 1 M investment in the four housing markets (Germany, Spain, San Diego, and Dallas), in stocks, and bonds in comparison to inflation. Increases in index value, annual expenses and returns (compound return excluding inflation) are shown. Acquisition costs are accounted for in the first year.

V.2 Volatility Performance

The volatility of the final return depends on the susceptibility of its various components at the beginning of the investment, during the running period, and the termination costs. Relevant parameters are calculated and discussed hereinafter. This model aims to highlight the variances and risks should any of these cost factors change.

V.2.1 Volatility in Asset Prices

As discussed, the purchase of a house is done usually in one process and cannot be divided in parts. Therefore, the market conditions in both buying and selling real estate are essential for the overall return of the investment. In this study, disposing of the asset at an interval of $\pm 2\sigma$ equaling a probability of 95.45 % is calculated (see Table 3). It is noted that the risk can be reduced for wealthy investors when acquiring several pieces of real estate, in particular, in different markets at different times.

For stocks and bonds, the asset allocation can take place in pieces over a period of time reducing risk. This has already been applied in the model when buying stocks over 5 years. Even if the same may be applied to the selling process a single disposal at the end of the last year is shown. The change of $\pm 2\sigma$ was put in at the level of the final stock price without changes in dividends;

the latter being investigated in comparison to changes in rental income below.

Table 3: Volatility Calculation at a lower Return of 2 Standard Deviations

This table shows the disposal values, which were altered for a decrease of 2 standard deviations of the simulated sale value after 20 years and the reduced return rate exponentially decreased. The %-difference of the ROI after 20 years was calculated.

		Germany	Spain	San Diego	Dallas	MSCI world	FTSE bonds
	Index return	2.15%	3.76%	5.02%	3.33%	4.70%	4.21%
Proceeds	return (-2 sigma)	1.93%	3.39%	4.53%	3.00%	4.24%	3.80%
	gain / loss	-14%	-15%	-18%	-11%	-16%	-31%

V.2.2 Volatility by Variation of Running Costs

Deviations from the unaltered model in relation to changes of property taxes, maintenance costs or rents are calculated (see Table 4) and accordingly visualized based on the incremental annual %-change of total return (see Figure 8). To highlight the differences the %-increase of *net* return (profit) on capital is shown after a 20-year investment period.

Table 4: Change in ROI altering Costs and Periodical Income

This table shows the change of annual return when costs and rents increase by a constant 10%, respectively. No property tax is assumed for MSCI world and FTSE bonds. No coupon is derived from FTSE bonds (performance index).

		Germany	Spain	San Diego	Dallas	MSCI world	FTSE bonds
	Real return incl. Income	2.04%	3.87%	4.63%	4.75%	4.80%	1.99%
Property tax	return (+ 10 %)	2.02%	3.78%	4.55%	4.55%		
	gain / loss	-0.9%	-3.4%	-2.5%	-6.6%		
Maintainance	return (+ 10 %)	1.96%	3.79%	4.58%	4.67%	4.77%	1.97%
	gain / loss	-5.1%	-3.1%	-1.8%	-2.7%	-0.8%	-1.5%
Rent	return (+ 10 %)	2.33%	4.32%	4.99%	5.44%	5.03%	
	gain / loss	15.2%	14.4%	10.6%	18.8%	6.9%	

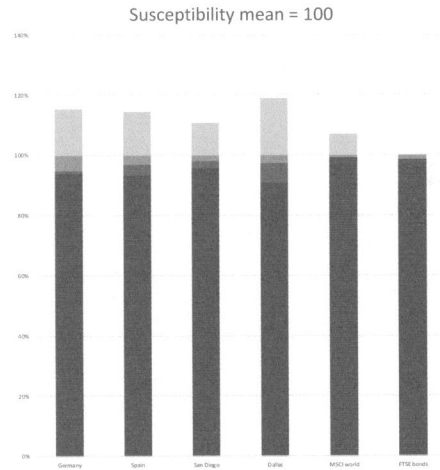

Susceptibility mean = 100

Figure 8: Changes of Net Return after 20 Years

This figure shows changes in net returns for altering costs and periodical income. The 100 % base line refers to the unaltered model (rent increases enhanced return, increase in costs lower the return), changes in costs are added linearly. The scale is set from 0 intentionally.

Volatility and susceptibility to changes of parameters in the underlying model have been discussed and quantified. A more comprehensive view of risks can be taken by quantifying the long-term interdependence of the markets and asset classes. This estimation of the risk *among* the investments in a portfolio is given by calculating the correlation matrix of the returns based on the house price indices and the MSCI world stock and FTSE world bond indices, respectively. A subsequential shock simulation estimates the specific impact of an unforeseen event on the long-term returns.

Table 5 shows that all correlation coefficients are below 0.5 for all markets. Hence, the investments are relatively uncoupled from each other except a negative link between Dallas and the FTSI bonds. The real estate market is relatively uncoupled from the stock market (less than 0.35). Stock markets and volatile housing markets especially like San Diego are – weakly - positively linked, bond markets mostly negatively. Only German housing shows a negative correlation to both bonds and stocks. In between the housing markets analyzed, San Diego is loosely – below 0.5 - correlated with Spain and Dallas, respectively.

Table 5: Asset Correlation

This table shows the correlation matrix between market index returns (all available years). Stock markets and volatile housing markets especially like San Diego are positively linked, bond markets mostly negatively. German housing shows a negative correlation to both bonds and stocks.

	Germany	Spain	San Diego	Dallas	MSCI world	FTSE bonds
Germany	1.000	-0.279	-0.270	0.447	-0.229	-0.141
Spain		1.000	0.478	-0.001	0.044	0.282
San Diego			1.000	0.424	0.344	-0.161
Dallas				1.000	0.027	-0.595
MSCI world					1.000	0.131
FTSE bonds						1.000

Using the identical scale, from Figure 9 it becomes clearly visible that, Germany and Spain show an even lower variation of the housing market with the stock market. Although at a low level, slightly higher and positive correlation coefficients are obtained for Spain and San Diego. This reflects the effect of the housing crisis of 2009 on these two markets, whereas Germany and Dallas were unaffected. It has to be noted that due to the availability of data the complete calculation is based on different durations of 44 years for Germany, 24 for Spain, 32 for San Diego, and 20 years for Dallas, respectively. For the purpose of comparison, the 20-year values are provided showing the same trend (see Table 6).

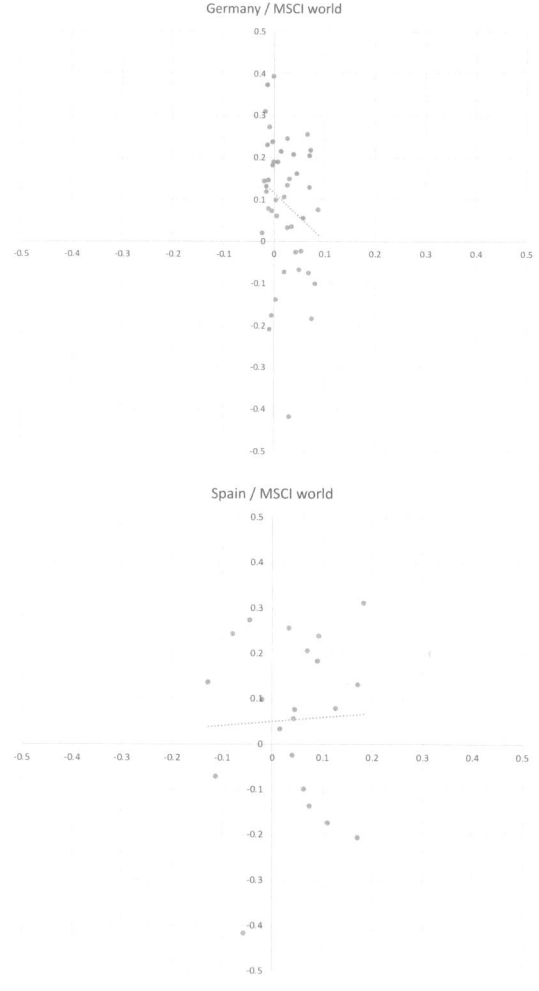

Figure 9: Correlation between MSCI world and German and Spanish House Price Index Returns

Annual index returns are plotted against each other, including trendline correlation. Identical scaling for comparison.

Table 6: Asset correlation (20 years)

Correlation matrix as above for 1999-2019.

	Germany	Spain	San Diego	Dallas	MSCI world	FTSE bonds
Germany	1.000	-0.319	-0.208	0.447	-0.042	-0.281
Spain		1.000	0.462	-0.001	0.015	0.316
San Diego			1.000	0.424	0.339	-0.044
Dallas				1.000	0.027	-0.595
MSCI world					1.000	-0.089
FTSE bonds						1.000

V.4 Shock Simulation

The simulated 50% shock over 3 years decreases the overall return by 3 to 10% equaling a loss of 65,000 to 244,000 of the 1 million investment after 20 years before taxation (see Table 7 and Figure 10).

Table 7: Shock Simulation Data

This table shows consequences of a 3-year, 50% decrease in rental income and dividends, respectively, whilst maintaining the expense scheme is shown as proceeds of a 1 M investment after 20 years. The percentage of lost return is given.

	Germany	Spain	San Diego	Dallas	MSCI world	FTSE bonds
Return w/o shock	1.50	2.14	2.47	2.53	2.55	1.48
Return w/shock	1.43	2.00	2.35	2.29	2.47	1.48
% Return lost	-4.3%	-6.4%	-5.2%	-9.6%	-3.4%	0.0%
	Germany	Spain	San Diego	Dallas	MSCI world	FTSE bonds
Return w/o shock	1.50	2.14	2.47	2.53	2.55	1.48
Return w/shock	1.43	2.00	2.35	2.29	2.47	1.48
% Return lost	-4.3%	-6.4%	-5.2%	-9.6%	-3.4%	0.0%

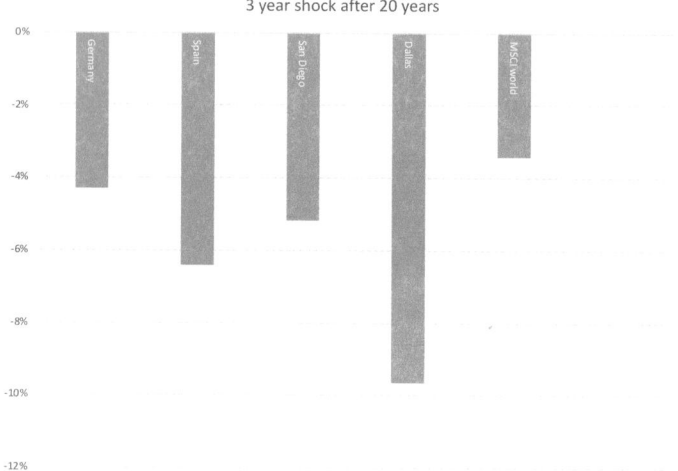

Figure 10: Shock Simulation Graph

This figure shows the return differences in % for a 3-year shock after 20 years. Because the FTSE world bond index does not carry dividends but fixed coupons no change in total returns is observed.

VI. DISCUSSION

VI.1 Markets in General

Stocks and bonds as widely accessible and liquid markets are the backbone of the financial world. In contrast, housing markets are local and susceptible to specific particularities such as law/regulation, language, or taxation. To overcome this obstacle, this study focused on large and transparent markets. Personal considerations, often linked to culture, play a large and often overlooked role. Consequently, for "western" investors North America and Europe will be the main target markets, although South America or South Africa could be considered as potential alternatives.

While investing in an index fund of either stocks or bonds covering all aspects of the market, the purchase of a house narrows down the allocation to a specific object. House price indices and its analysis provide a general smoothened overview of the market and may only indicate the broad direction of the individual investment. Accordingly, several investment criteria above and beyond the pure return performance have to be taken into account.

VI.2 Openness

No market for investment is more open and liquid than the stock market. Index and company data is readily available in multiple formats and languages. Stocks can be traded worldwide within a fraction of a second. Transaction costs are close to zero and became nearly irrelevant for a long-term investor.

Due to its high turnover U.S. real estate markets are liquid and readily accessible. The English language makes it easy to derive relevant information. Thus, information asymmetries can be reduced.

The JLL transparency tiers (Global Real Estate Transparency Index, 2020) of all four countries are transparent to high with ranks ranging from 2 to 19 out of 99 reported countries. Information about the fiscal side in Spain, however, remains opaque. Limited data is available in Spanish language whereas in English almost no reliable information can be obtained. Foreign investors are well dependent on a trustful partner such as a real estate agent. To some extent the same may also apply to foreign speaking investors in Germany.

VI.3 Returns

All returns were calculated using continuously compound returns exponential functions also including rents and expenses. Consideration is needed in scenarios of decoupling inflation with house values. Especially in long-term analyses or inflated environments rents and maintenance costs may lag house prices, whereas property taxes – with the notable exception of California – are linked to real valuations.

Acquisition related costs were spread over the investment period to generate annual returns. In Europe these expenses are paid mainly by the buyer, in the U.S. mostly by the seller. For monitoring the course of the investment these costs were booked round-trip in the first year. In this study, it is demonstrated that for investment horizons less than 5 years real estate lags stocks, bonds and even a classical savings account. In contrast, returns for any longer period show the superior benefits; the only exception being Germany where a bond investment is more attractive at any given realistic time horizon. Stocks as an asset class keep up with the returns of San Diego and Dallas showing similar returns after 20 and 40 years, respectively.

Whereas dividend returns for stocks may be reinvested immediately within its asset class, excess rental income cannot readily. For comparison, the presented model includes compound interest at each the calculated asset return rate. Moving regular real estate proceeds into the stock market can thus keep high compounded interest returns by reducing risk at the same time through the allocation of capital over (at least) two asset classes.

Despite having climbed 31% since its low in 2010, the Spanish home price index of 2019 is still 17% below its record level of 2007 even in nominal terms. This indicates that real estate returns in Spain may be underestimated despite the long 20-year period investigated. In contrast, the other three market indices rose a higher 36% to 44% in the same 6-year period from an uninflated level for Germany and Dallas.

VI.4 Acquisition Costs and Property Taxes

For long-term oriented investors acquisition costs both for real estate and stocks – even being significant for the prior asset class – are of less importance. Depot fees for stocks and managing fees especially for index funds decreased enormously in the past, approaching and even reaching 0%. On the other hand, property taxes on real estate did not show this reduction. On the contrary they even have upward pressure like the additional bonds being introduced at the U.S. county level being added to the tax rate (e.g. school bonds) or the ongoing discussion about the revamping of the German property tax system.

For an average citizen the property tax *amount* for his home and its ration to his available income is his most important figure. In 2016 an average Californian house owner paid USD 4,783 in property tax (AttomData, 2020), whereas the median family in Texas owed USD 4,660, almost the same amount. On the contrary, as an investor the property tax *rate* is relevant. In California the median rate is 0.77% from the cited reference (AttomData, 2020; similar to a 20-year mean of 0.78% in the presented San Diego metro area example) and Texas is

1.83% (Smartasset, 2020). On a 1 M investment, this results in USD 7,800 for California to USD 18,320 per year in Texas and even USD 19,920 for Dallas.

In California proposition 13 reduces the 20-year average property tax rate by roughly 1/3 of the – for U.S. conditions already low – 1.1%. For any subsequent period, the property tax rate will fall further. Therefore, California plays out its advantage to Texas in the long run.

Individual taxes consist of a major drag on the return of the investment. These tax rates highly depend on the nature of the investment entity – it could be, e.g., an individual, a company, a REIT or even an endowment. It should be noted that in most countries annual returns like dividends and rents are taxed differently than capital gains.

In some jurisdictions like Switzerland long-term investments are even exempted from capital gains tax (Kanton Zug, 2020); dividends, however, are fully taxable at the income tax rate. In the U.S. the capital gains tax rate depends on the regular income hence the financial status of the investor himself (Internal Revenue Service, 2019). Therefore, a concluding calculation with the long-term capital gains tax component cannot be provided. Still, suggesting a 25% reduction of the investment's return does sound reasonable for most developed countries.

VI.5 Running Costs

Maintenance and running costs are essential. Utilities like water, garbage disposal and natural gas are excluded in both income and costs (German "Kaltmiete"). Depending on the location homeowner association (HOA) fees may apply as well as, e.g., expenses for landscaping. Moreover, roof and furnace replacements, landscape and pavement renewals, and general repairs are significant outflows of capital on a non-regular but repeated schedule. There are several estimates to calculate maintenance expenses (HomeUnion, 2020):

a) "50% Rule – 50% of the rental property income should be set aside for maintenance, taxes, insurance, etc."

b) "1% Rule – 1% of how much the home is worth at the time of purchase is how much to set aside yearly for maintenance."

c) Square Footage Formula - $1 for every square foot per year

d) 5x Rule - 1.5 times the monthly rent

The 50% rule would yearly allocate 2-3% of the investment towards maintenance, the 1% rule up to 1%, the square footage formula (e.g., Dallas 4 properties 2500 sqft each = 10,0000 USD) 1% and the 5x rule (5% / 12 * 1.5) 2/3 of one percent annually. These rules imply property taxes which have been discussed and calculated separately. To address maintenance costs, it is generally assumed that 50% of the investment applies to structures and 50% towards the lot. For California, land prices are significantly higher for which a correction-factor of 2/3 was applied. In a real-world investment this factor needs to be adjusted accordingly, e.g., for several Spanish coastal and island regions. The costs are spread on 50 years. For the given EUR 1 M investment this equals EUR 5,000 annually.

Long-term remodeling or replacement expenses (e.g. roof replacement, a new heater or repairs) add to the maintainance costs and inceasing Capex. To illustrate three known examples of single-family units are analyzed since the date of purchase (see Table 8).

Table 8: Annual Maintenance Costs

This table shows an actual example of associated costs of three properties – two in California, one in central Europe – since purchase (own data), annualized to 20 years, not indexed

	House 1	House 2	House 3
Location	CA	CA	EU
Years of ownership	13	12	7
Value ('000)	3,200	2,500	800
Roof replacement	1,923		429
Furnace replacement	615		
Utilities replacement	308	42	214
Painting, carpet		1,000	
Structures	38		4,000
Yard	538	1,000	
HOA		6,000	
Landscaping	2,200	5,000	
Insurances	1,800	1,800	500
Annual maintenance	0.23%	0.59%	0.64%

The costs are calculated on a yearly basis and are lower than as seen in the calculation used. A few remodeling expenses are included like a new roof, the groves reshaping and a replacement of a winter garden but no major work on the fundamental structures. Adding up these components, the formula used in this study is applicable in a real-world environment. To predict and control the cost structure an inspection before investing in real estate is essential.

It needs to be noted that the HOA fees can be of substantial importance to the return of the investment as they usually are in the range of a few USD 100 per month. At USD 200 times two properties HOA fees alone reduce the total return by about 0.5% or USD 140,000 in 20 years for 1 M investment.

VI.6 Risks

A variety of risk factors were assembled and are discussed henceforth focusing on real estate investments, in particular of the selected markets (see Table 9).

Table 9: Overview of Risk Factors and Advantages

	Real Estate	Stocks	Bonds
RISKS	Natural disasters	Third party risk	Third party risks (limited)
	Access	Bankruptcies	Bankruptcies (limited)
	Local politics (taxes, law)	Fraud	Local politics (taxes, law)
	Investment locked in longterm	Fluctuations	Inflation risks
	Enviromental		
ADVANTAGES	Stable returns	Flexible, adjustable	Liquid, quick
	Predictable	Liquid, quick	Predictable
	Refugee place	Inflation-safe	Stable returns
	Inflation-safe		

In the real estate market *natural disasters* are unavoidable. For the markets studied, earthquakes and fire hazards in California and hurricanes for Texas are well-known. Some risk can be covered by insurance at cost. If a larger investment is considered – like the 1 M as studied – two houses could be acquired which should not be located closely.

Market access to the real estate investment is also a risk and cost factor. Terror related or pandemic travel restrictions are newer obstacles to consider. If rented out a well-standing relationship to the tenant is helpful for solving unexpected issues like carrying out smaller maintenance-related tasks or communication with local authorities like for obtaining permits (e.g., for cutting down a rotten tree).

In this study two markets in the EUR-zone are compared with 2 metro areas in the USD region, and thus, being subject to foreign *exchange rate* (FX) risk. This risk plays out in both ways wherever the investor or the investment is located. It is assumed both risks to be equal, so no further consideration is applied hereto. Inflation numbers are similar – besides a slightly lower figure for Germany – thus justifying masking this effect and being proved by the relatively constant EUR-USD long-term exchange rate.

As shown in Figure 11, over 35 years from 1975 (calculated) to 2020 the EUR / USD FX rate held steady at about 1.2 indicating FX risks can be mostly neglected for a long-term investment. However, it should be noted that an investment in times of, e.g., elevated values of EUR / USD = 1.6 alone lead to FX gains of 45 % when selling at EUR / USD 1.1 and vice versa. A FX risk minimizing strategy could be designed by gradually exchanging the initial funds or proceeds of the foreign-currency denominated real estate property over a longer period of time.

EUR / USD FX Rates

Figure 11: EUR / USD FX Rates

This figure shows the historical chart of the EUR / USD exchange rate for the period 1975-2020 including trend line (source: Bloomberg)

In addition, there a several ***risks at disposal*** of a property. Common stocks and bonds are readily disposable at the current market price assuming a negligible amount is sold in reference to the average trading volume. In these asset classes a selling strategy – inversely to the buying scheme - spread over several years can be selected to further eliminate risks. For real estate not only the opaque market price of the property has to be taken into account but also the market condition as a whole alters the selling price as well as the duration of the disposal process. Depending on being a seller's or buyer's market sometimes resulting in bidding wars which may drive prices even higher. On the other hand, fire sales reduce returns on investments. Furthermore, it is not uncommon for expensive properties to be on the market for a longer time. San Diego and Dallas being sizeable markets with a high volume of sales, especially at the median price levels. For luxury investments the turnover and the flexibility of the market is reduced, so that buying two or more properties at a lower price rather than one luxury house attract more liquid-oriented investors. This approach also enables spreading the risk while increasing the workload, e.g., twice the probability of a failed furnace, handling two sets of tax payments etc.

Disposal risks in pricing are similar for all four housing markets, whereas San Diego is being slightly elevated and in line with the MSCI world. Even at 2 standard deviations or 95.45 %, the risk at around 15% seems to be worth taken, given the overall returns of these investments. Despite fluctuating less than the other assets, bonds carry a higher risk on disposal as the return is comparatively inferior.

Determining the overall return changes in rents, running costs and the entire *cost structure* have to be carefully monitored. Especially, Spain with its high property taxes is susceptible for lower returns should these duties being raised. However, its impact on the personal tax level cannot be foreseen. A 10% increase was calculated to result in a decrease of 3.4% of total return after 20 years. Different outcomes can be estimated using the volatility (tables 3 and 4) in the results section of this study. Changes in maintenance costs have a substantial impact in Germany because of the comparatively (Turkish Statistical Institute, 2020) low yield in rent. All changes, however, are well below 10% in ROI after 20 years.

Increasing the rents directly adds to the bottom line especially where the real return before rents is negative. For the stock market 10 % higher dividends lead to an increase of 6.9 %. It has to be noted, though, that higher payouts lower the stock values.

The simulated *economic shock* is more severe than experienced outside wartimes to demonstrate consequences of a heavy impact. Recessions likely will lead to disruptions minor to this simulation. Even at this magnitude long-term effects after 20 years are less than 10%. Markets with high rents like Dallas are more susceptible than low-return areas such as Germany. The stock market is impacted by lower dividends. In a shock / recession environment, the risk of insolvencies of companies adds to losses in dividend yields. The bond market with its given coupons is shielded from any impact as long as governments keep being solvent.

In contrast to the EUR-zone and the U.S., Switzerland shows lower long-term *inflation* of 0.45% (Bundesamt für Statistik, 2020) or Turkey a significantly higher inflation rate of 14.8% (Turkish Statistical Institute, 2020) during the period of 1999-2019. Studying these markets, the difference in inflation would have needed to be considered. Compensating for FX a hedging strategy may be applied. However, hedging costs easily eat up any returns. A potential strategy could be buying one property each in Europe and the U.S. leveling out currency risks for an investment based on a mean FX rate and reducing these risks for the investor by half.

Price volatility at the stock market is comparatively high. Particularly, investments from/to a bubble or burst market may distort even long-term revenues. During the period from 1999-2019 the MSCI world base returns of 2.6% annually is mainly the result of an exaggerated index value of 1421 at the height of the Dot-com bubble. For this analysis, this peak was smoothed by linear averaging for 1999 on a 10-year period resulting in a return of 4.3%. Narrowing down this window to +/- 3 years, the return reduces again to 3.8%. Also being true for the real estate market but eclipsed by the stock market, this highlights the importance of market timing. However, in contrast of buying a property, stocks can be purchased in small units. A risk-reducing strategy for this 20-year example for stocks may be investing 20% of the capital annually over a period of 5 years while maintaining the balance on a risk-free Bunds or U.S. treasuries account.

Bankruptcy is another source of risk. Whereas the bankruptcy risks of stocks due to the broad base of the MSCI index itself are minimal – i.e. a bankruptcy of a single company in the 1600 index portfolio stock portfolio equals 0.0625 %, certificates based on this index cannot be seen as such. This was shown by the downfall of Lehman Brothers in September 2008 (Amadeo, 2020) where certificates issued by this investment bank became worthless. A risk-reducing strategy may be dividing the investment to several certificates issued by a variety of banks. The same applies to the bond market although bankruptcies of governments are less likely reflected by lower risk premiums. Direct investment in government bonds rather than in ETFs lower the risks even further.

Relative Risks in between Markets

Relative risks between the housing and the stock market are low. Effects of the 2009 housing bubble can be seen in Spain and in San Diego resulting in a higher positive correlation to the stock market. Despite the crash, the correlation in Spain is at 0.04 well below 1.

Thus, risks for these markets are slightly higher than for Germany and Dallas. Therefore, an equal allocation of assets between real estate investments and stock holdings helps reduce risks. This study bases the stock market analysis on the MSCI world index. Local dependencies may exist. As an example, before the US housing crisis elevated house prices enticed consuming more which in turn spurred the local economy. Investing in local stocks also reduces the exposure to changes in FX-rates.

The estimated risk for the German housing market can be considered as stable, while San Diego shows more volatile variation, however, is still lower compared to the international stock market (see Figure 12).

Germany / San Diego

Figure 12: Correlation between Germany and San Diego Indexes

This figure shows a plot of German against San Diego home price index returns. Scaling according to the MSCI world plots.

Relative risk thus is negligible besides effects such as environmental disasters and political disruptions which lie outside of this study.

In the single-family house market legal procedures are rather standardized and regulated by law. Still, *legal risks* remain. According to the National Association of Realtors (National Association of Realtors, 2007), breaches of fiduciary duty accounted for the largest number of lawsuits, followed by failure to disclose, misrepresentation, or the misstating of some material feature of the property. Contamination risks like groundwater contamination, carbon monoxide, lead-based paint, and mold exist but are limited.

Law varies even within one country and one state, e.g., in Santa Clara, California the buyer can demand repairs before the sale is closed, whereas in San Diego the buyer may only ask for. Also, when renting out the investment property legal aspects need to be considered, e.g., if tenant refuses to move.

VI.7 Long Term Perspective

In real estate initial costs are substantial (all round trip costs are shown in the first year as the exit costs of a real estate investment are accountable from day one). Unsurprisingly, an investment horizon in single-family real estate of less than 5 years is unfavorable for the four targets discussed. Given the acquisition costs, a similar result will occur in almost all markets. For short-term investments stock-based real estate assets or REITs may be a valuable alternative. Even here, issue premiums and other fund related costs can be a major factor.

While returns in San Diego, Dallas and Spain surpass inflation – based on the averaged figure used for MSCI – until about year 4 and for Germany in year 7, all markets perform similarly.

When accounted for proposition 13 in California the effect in the calculation appears to be negative for the first years – not in reality where the tax cannot exceed 1% plus approved bonds – as this effect was normalized for year 10 during the analysis. In the long run, however, the consequences are clearly obvious. Referring to a USD 1.7 million real-world investment in 2007 (house #1) the property tax rate in year 13 runs at USD 25,000. Instead of being comparatively valued on the market at roughly USD 3.5+ million, the assessed value stands at less than USD 2.0 M. These tax savings account for USD 13,000 in year 13 alone. Albeit not all California houses appreciated similarly the shown difference clearly highlights the advantage of a real estate investment in the U.S.

It should be added that the remote state of Hawaii might be considered as an alternative in terms of low property tax running at 0.25 % to 0.33% (SmartAsset, 2020). Still, the MSCI World eclipses all studied investments. Only California is able to catch up after more than three decades.

Looking further down the road a very long investment horizon of 40 years is presented in Figure 13. To illustrate the overall yield, an overview is shown being extended from the previous calculations based on the same data sources. Using the model of San Diego, proposition 13 reduces annual taxation of the 1 M investment in year 40 from 171,000 to 24,000 equaling a tax rate of 0.15% from the initial 1.1%.

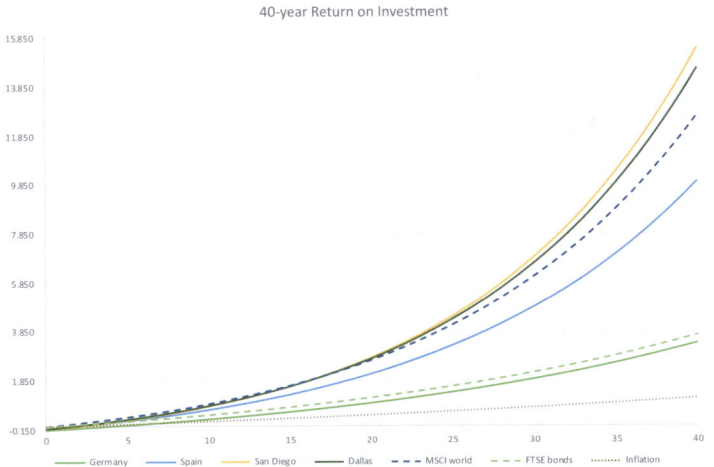

Figure 13: 40-year Long-Term Returns

This figure shows the historical return over a period of 40 years. Total return calculated accordingly the model given extended to 40 years. Corrected for CA proposition 13.

Initial costs are no longer substantial and can hardly been seen anymore. The low property taxes of San Diego and the higher rents in Dallas, respectively, play out their advantages keeping up with and eventually exceeding the stock market. Only Spain can follow its U.S. counterparts. However, Spanish property taxation as discussed is a challenging number to predict for this long investment horizon. Being safe and predictable, investments in German real estate or in international bonds lack chances which has been already demonstrated in all other examples.

Especially for an extreme horizon additional care has to be applied on the impacts of any investment exponentially eclipsing long-term inflation. Any further investor to come when disposing the assets has to deliver the capital needed. Unless it is an exchange of investments funds have to come from earned income like labor. In a low-interest environment credit is readily available at low costs disguising the issue repaying the mortgages similar to the 2008 housing bubble. On the other hand, inflation figures are likely to be understated. Such will limit both the risk of the investment and the return relative to inflation. Return and real inflation cannot be decoupled forever.

VI.8 Taxes

Individual taxes are excluded in this study as they are dependent of the investor's jurisdiction with the exception of the Spanish property tax due by any property owner. Two main classes of duties needed to be taken into account: yearly income taxes and capital gains at the end of the investment period with the former implying the disadvantage of lost compound interest. For real estate, running costs are deductible as is – in some jurisdictions – the depreciation of the building itself. Offsetting parts of the rental proceeds, income taxes are deferred towards the disposal of the property.

Total 20-year Inflation at 47% reduces the net return for Germany from 0.96 to 0.35 M and for San Diego from 2.79 to 1.49 M for a 20-year 1 M investment. As taxes are applied on nominal rather than on inflation adjusted values they further limit the real return of the investment. Assuming a 25% capital gains tax rate for the example given above, net returns narrow down further to

0.22 M for Germany and 1.08 M for San Diego, not even accounting for estate taxes. Careful long-term tax planning strategies are thus essential (Jeffers, 2007).

VI.9 Additional Considerations

Even in our tech-based and interconnected world real estate is still local. The German term "Immobilien" translating to "not movable" says just that. There are major consequences. On the positive side, owning real estate provides security to the investor in a broad sense. Countries will guarantee safety to its people where they live- as much as they are able to. As a long-term investor, the possibility for applying citizenship is a welcomed perspective or at least providing peace of mind having a place to escape to, should unforeseen major events happen. On the contrary, real estate cannot be shifted from one place to another should unfavorable developments evolve like tax hikes, unstable political movements, natural disasters or even wars. Thus, and if affordable, real estate investments should not be located in one area exclusively. These factors need to be weighted in as well as costs and, often overlooked, the time to manage the properties including extensive travel, e.g., having already invested in the San Diego market, Dallas is a further 2-day drive, whereas a second investment in Las Vegas, Nevada would be much closer.

VII. CONCLUSION AND OUTLOOK

The studied model of a long-term investment compared four housing markets on two continents, the stock, and the bond market reveal significant differences in returns and risks. Over a 20-year period the housing markets of San Diego and Dallas matched the outperformance of the stock market over bonds and the remaining markets of Germany and Spain. The returns of the latter, however, fall not far behind the leading group enabling an investment in the Iberian country for the purpose of geographic risk distribution. The housing market of Germany cannot even match the returns of the world-wide government bond market. At the end of the 20-year investment period, all six markets generated both positive nominal and real returns.

All gains were shown to be surprisingly robust to changes in returns, costs and even shocks. A significant 2-Sigma variation of the net yield – which in the case of single-family homes correlates to the rent - alters the final return at mid to low teens of % after 20 years; with the notable exception of bonds. The model is robust to

10% increases of property taxes and maintenance costs lowering returns at low to mid-single digits of %.

The disadvantages of the housing markets towards stocks and bonds being local, less liquid, mandating a long-term view, exposed to local politics and environmental risk factors are compensated by stable inflation-safe returns, non-existent bankruptcy risks and personal safeguards offering a safe haven not limited to financial aspects.

This study reveals that of the four markets studies real estate in particular in the San Diego area of California emerges as a suitable target both in terms of return and safety. When focusing on Europe, the Spanish real estate market looks attractive for investors. The remainder of the capital should be invested in stocks like in funds linked to the MSCI world index. As with all types of investments, risks are attached to each market and asset class. These should be minimized by spreading the investment accordingly. In conclusion, allocating long-term capital into real estate proves to be more attractive than widely assumed.

VII. Conclusion and Outlook

This work provides well-represented examples of real estate investing in the Western and Northern hemisphere. Further research may extend this approach towards other countries in Asia including Japan, Australia, South America or even Africa with deviating environments of culture, demographics and law. Additional work could involve the commercial side of the corresponding real estate markets and turning towards REIT structures including leverage analysis. Subsequent studies to optimize tax structures may enhance the robustness of the model further. Finally, environmental effects of climate change on the long-term return of real estate investments need to be analyzed.

BIBLIOGRAPHY

Literature

Agatha E. Jeffers, I. E. (2007). Impact of Taxes on Foreign Investment in U.S. Real Estate. International Journal of Business Strategy, VII, 117-130.

Bana Abuzayed, N. A.-F. (2020). Co-movement across european stock and real estate markets. International Review of Economics and Finance, 69 89–208.

Baur, D. a. (2010). Is Gold a Hedge or a Safe Haven? An Analysis of Stocks, Bonds and Gold. Financial Review, 45: 217-229.

Bowen, H. V. (1989). Investment and empire in the later eighteenth century: East India stockholding, 1756-1791. Economic History Review, 2nd ser. XLII, 2, pp. 186-206.

Carolina Fugazza, M. G. (2007). Investing for the Long-run in European Real Estate. J Real Estate Finan Econ, 34:35–80.

Cay Oertel, T. G. (2019). US real estate as target assets for European investors. Journal of Property Investment & Finance, Vol. 37 No. 4, 398-404.

Christina Christou, R. G. (2018). Do house prices hedge inflation in the US? A quantile cointegration approach.

International Review of Economics and Finance, 54: 15–26.

Chyi Lin Lee, M.-L. L. (2014). Do European Real Estate Stocks Hedge Inflation? International Journal of Strategic Property Management , 18(2): 178–197.

Eddie C.M. Hui, J. C. (2016). Are international securitized property markets converging or diverging? Physica A, 446: 1-10.

Edwards, C. (1906). The Oldest Laws in the World: Being an Account of the Hammurabi Code and the Sinaitic Legislation. London: Watt's & Co.

Eugene Farmer, W. S. (1977). Asset Returns And Inflation. Journal of Financial Economics, 5, 15-146.

G. Jason Goddard, B. M. (2012). Real Estate Investment. Heidelberg, Dordrecht, London, New York: Springer.

Graham, B. (1949). The Intelligent Investor. New York: Harper & Brothers.

Haberman, C. (2016, 10 17). The California Ballot Measure That Inspired a Tax Revolt. Ney York Times.

Ibbotson, R. G. (2010). The Importance of Asset Allocation. Financial Analysts Journal, 66:2.

J. Sa-Aadu, J. S. (2010). On the Portfolio Properties of Real Estate in Good Times and Bad Times. REAL ESTATE ECONOMICS, 3: pp. 529–565.

Jadevicius, A. (2019). Real estate portfolios – the case for globally diversified core property funds. Journal of Property Investment & Finance, 38 No. 1, pp. 82-86.

Jian Yang, Y. Z. (2012). Asymmetric Correlation and Volatility Dynamics among Stock, Bond, and Securitized Real Estate Markets. J Real Estate Finan Econ, 45:491–521.

Luca Begatti, C. M. (2018). Assessing housing market dynamics across a sample of European cities. Copenhagen: Copenhagen Business School.

Massimo Guidolin, M. P. (2020). The Predictability of Real Estate Excess Returns: An Out-of-Sample Economic Value Analysis. J Real Estate Finan Econ.

Nikolaos Antonakakisa, R. G. (2017). Has the correlation of inflation and stock prices changed in the United States over the last two centuries? Research in International Business and Finance, 42, 1-8.

Richa Pandey, V. M. (2019). Sub-optimal behavioural biases and decision theory in real estate. International Journal of Housing Markets and Analysis, 12 No. 2, 330-348.

Richter, J., Thomas, M., & F (et.al, 1991)üss, R. (2011). German Real Estate Return Distributions : Is There Anything Normal? Journal of Real Estate Portfolio Management, 17 (2). 161-179.

Stephen Ross, R. Z. (1991). Risk and Return in Real Estate. *Journal of Real EstateFinance and Economics*, 4:175-190.

Semer, S. L. (2009). A Brief History of US REITs. Canadian Tax Journal, 4: 960-971.

Stephen Ross, R. Z. (1991). Risk and Return in Real Estate. Journal of Real EstateFinance and Economics, 4:175-190.

Talmud. (200). תַּלְמוּד. Talmud 173, Jeb. 63a; D. 463.

Tien Foo Sing, Z. Y. (2013). Time-varying correlations between stock and direct real estate returns. Journal of Property Investment & Finance, 31 No. 2, 179-195.

V, Shobha C. (2017, 11). A STUDY ON GOLD AS A SAFER INVESTMENT ALTERNATIVE. International Journal of Research.

Yunus, N. (2020). Time-varying linkages among gold, stocks, bonds and real estate. The Quarterly Review of Economics and Finance, 77: 165–185.

Other Sources

Amadeo, K. (2020, 04 16). Retrieved from The Balance: https://www.thebalance.com/lehman-brothers-collapse-causes-impact-4842338

Andalucia-Lawyers. (2016). Retrieved from https://www.andalucia-lawyers.com/spanish-wealth-tax-2016/

ARD. (2020, 11 6). ARD boerse. Retrieved from bo-erse.ard.de/

AttomData. (2020). Mortgagecalculator. Retrieved from https://www.mortgagecalculator.org/helpful-advice/property-taxes.php

Brainsre. (2020). Retrieved from https://brainsre.news/en/the-lowdown-on-the-rental-market-in-spain/

Brent W. Ambrose, P. L. (2001). REIT Organizational Structure and Operating Characteristics. University of Pennsylvania.

Bundesamt für Statistik. (2020). Retrieved from https://fxtop.com/

Bundesamt, S. (2019). Retrieved from https://www.destatis.de/

Bundesfinanzministerium. (2019, 06). Vergleich.de. Retrieved from https://www.vergleich.de/grundsteuer.html

Bundesfinanzministerium. (2019, 6 21). Retrieved from https://www.bundesfinanzministerium.de/Content/DE/FAQ/2019-06-21-faq-die-neue-grundsteuer.html

Census, U. (2020). US Census. Retrieved from census.gov

Chainstoreage. (2020, 8 3). Retrieved from https://chainstoreage.com/plunge-retail-rents-continue-fifth-avenue-and-other-luxury-shopping-sites

Dasinvestment. (2020). Retrieved from https://www.dasinvestment.com/bundesverfassungsgericht-was-aenderungen-bei-der-grundsteuer-fuer-eigentuemer-und-mieter-bedeuten-1/?page=2

Development, U. D. (2016). U.S. Department of Housing and Urban Development. Retrieved from https://www.huduser.gov/portal/publications/pdf/SanDiegoCA-comp-16.pdf

Development, U. D. (2018). U.S. Department of Housing and Urban Development. Retrieved from https://www.huduser.gov/portal/publications/pdf/DallasTX-comp-17.pdf

Dunlap, D. W. (2000). Commercial Real Estate; Cartier Spruces Up to Show Off Its Jewels in Style. New York: New York Times.

Equalization, C. S. (2019). Retrieved from https://www.boe.ca.gov/proptaxes/pdf/pub29.pdf

Equalization, C. S. (2020). Retrieved from https://www.boe.ca.gov/proptaxes/decline-in-value/

Eurostat. (2020). Eurostat. Retrieved from ec.europa.eu

Eurostat. (2020). Eurostat. Retrieved from
https://ec.europa.eu/eurostat/

Fed, S. L. (2020). Retrieved from
https://fred.stlouisfed.org/series/PSAVERT.

Fed, S. L. (2020). St. Louis Fed. Retrieved from
https://fred.stlouisfed.org/series/DAXRSA

Fed, S. L. (2020). St. Louis Fed. Retrieved from
https://fred.stlouisfed.org/series/SDXRSA

Financial Times. (2016). Retrieved from
https://ftalphaville.ft.com/2016/09/30/2176379/recalling-
the-oktx-housing-bust-of-the-mid-1980s/

Germany Trade & Invest. (2020). Retrieved from
https://www.gtai.de/gtai-en/invest/investment-
guide/the-tax-system/taxation-of-property-65634

Global Real Estate Transparency Index. JLL. (2020).

Globalpropertyguide. (2020, 6 5). Retrieved from
https://www.globalpropertyguide.com/Europe/German
y/Buying-Guide

Globalpropertyguide. (2020). Retrieved from
https://www.globalpropertyguide.com/Europe/Spain/B
uying-Guide

Globalpropertyguide. (2020). Retrieved from
https://www.globalpropertyguide.com/Europe/Spain/re
nt-yields

Globalpropertyguide. (2020). Retrieved from https://www.globalpropertyguide.com/North-America/United-States/Buying-Guide

Globalpropertyguide. (2020). Retrieved from https://www.globalpropertyguide.com/North-America/United-States/Price-History

HomeUnion. (2020). Retrieved from https://www.homeunion.com/average-hidden-maintenance-costs-rental-property/

Hur, J. (2020). History of Investing. Retrieved from Be-Businessed: https://bebusinessed.com/history/history-of-investing/

Impuestos, F. (2020). Retrieved from https://www.fiscal-impuestos.com/impuesto-bienes-inmuebles-IBI.html

INE, I. N. (2020). Retrieved from https://fxtop.com/

INE. (2020). Instituto Nacional de Estadística. Retrieved from https://www.ine.es/

InfoSparks. (2020). Sandiegorealestatehunter. Retrieved from https://www.sandiegorealestatehunter.com/blog/san-diego-real-estate-market-statistics/

Internal Revenue Service. (2019). Investment Income and Expenses. Department of the Treasury.

Investment, D. (2019). Retrieved from https://www.dasinvestment.com/wohnkarte-2019-so-hoch-sind-mieten-und-renditen-in-deutschland/

ISI Emerging Markets Group. (2020). CEICdata. Retrieved from https://www.ceicdata.com/

Justetf. (2020). Retrieved from www.justetf.com/

Kanton Zug. (2020). Capital Gain Tax. Zug: Kanton Zug.

Macrotrends. (2020). Retrieved from https://www.macrotrends.net/2548/euro-dollar-exchange-rate-historical-chart

MSCI. (2020). Real Estate Market Size 2019. MSCI.

MSCI. (2020). Retrieved from https://www.msci.com/documents/10199/149ed7bc-316e-4b4c-8ea4-43fcb5bd6523

Myspanishresidency. (2020). Retrieved from https://www.myspanishresidency.com/taxes-spain/property-tax-spain/

National Association of Realtors. AE Magazine. (2007).

Realtors, D. (2020). Retrieved from https://deleonrealty.com/

reit.com. (2012). reit.com. Retrieved from Archive: https://web.archive.org/web/20121113221303/http://www.reit.com/timeline/timeline.php

Report on the Economic Well-Being of U.S. Households in 2018. Federal Reserve. (2019).

Santarelli, M. (2020). Noradarealestate. Retrieved from Mymetrotex: https://www.noradarealestate.com/blog/dallas-real-estate-market/

SEC. (2011). Real Estate Investment Trusts (REIT. Office of Investor Education and Advocacy.

Shiller, S. C. (2020). Retrieved from Yahoo Finance: https://finance.yahoo.com/chart/%5EDAXR/

Shiller, S. C. (2020). Retrieved from Yahoo finance: https://finance.yahoo.com/quote/%5ESDXR/

SmartAsset. (2020). Retrieved from https://smartasset.com/taxes/hawaii-property-tax-calculator

Smartasset. (2020). Retrieved from https://smartasset.com/taxes/texas-property-tax-calculator#WDQGB0YWvu

Spain, C. B. (2019, 11). Retrieved from https://howtobuyinspain.com/en/spain-property-market-2020/

Statista. (2020). Anzahl der verkauften Eigenheime in Deutschland nach Bundesländern 2018 . Retrieved from https://de.statista.com/statistik/daten/studie/793159/umfrage/anzahl-der-verkauften-eigenheime-in-deutschland-nach-bundeslaendern/

Statista. (2020). Statista. Retrieved from
https://www.statista.com/statistics/774644/park-from-
households-dear-in-spain/

Statistisches Bundesamt. (2020). Retrieved from
https://www.destatis.de/DE/Themen/Wirtschaft/Preise/
Verbraucherpreisindex/_inhalt.html

Sueddeutsche Zeitung. (2018, 8 8). Retrieved from
https://www.sueddeutsche.de/politik/kommunen-
dierfeld-sieben-gemeinden-erheben-keine-grundsteuer-
dpa.urn-newsml-dpa-com-20090101-180808-99-461844

Towncharts. (2020). Retrieved from
https://www.towncharts.com/Towncharts-Data-
Sources.html

Turkish Statistical Institute. (2020). Retrieved from
https://fxtop.com/

U.S. Bureau of Labor Statistics. (2020). Retrieved from
https://www.bls.gov/cpi/tables/supplemental-
files/historical-cpi-u-202009.pdf

US SEC. (2020). Retrieved from www.investor.gov/

VDP. (2020). VDP Research. Retrieved from
https://www.vdpresearch.de/

Vranjes, T. (2020, 10 13). KCET.org. Retrieved from
https://www.kcet.org/shows/the-first-angry-
man/proposition-13-under-increased-scrutiny-as-
california-faces-economic

Waymond Rodgers, T. G. (2017). Decision Making for Personal Investment. Basingstoke: Palgrave Macmillan.

Ycombinator. (2020). Retrieved from https://news.ycombinator.com/item?id=22399909

Zillow. (2020, 11 7). Retrieved from https://www.zillow.com/homes/?searchQueryState=%7B%22pagination%22%3A%7B%7D%2C%22usersSearchTerm%22%3A%221110%20Hidden%20Oaks%20Dr%20Cen-tral%20Menlo%20Park%20Menlo%20Park%20CA%2094025%22%2C%22mapBounds%22%3A%7B%22west%22%3A-122.19844669103622%2C%22east%22%22

Zillow. (2020). Zillow. Retrieved from zillow.com

SUPPLEMENTAL MATERIAL

Index Data (raw, normalized)

Table 10: Index Data

Raw index data of the four real estate markets, MSCI world and FTSE bonds, combination of the data sets and normalization to 1999 = 100 (source: see text)

	Germany			Spain			San Diego		Dallas		MSCI world		FTSE bonds	
1999 = 100	Index 1	Index 2	Combined	Index 1	Index 2 (m2)	Combined	Index	Normalized	Index	Normalized	Index	Normalized	Index	Normalized
31.12.1975	55		54								101	7		
31.12.1976	56		55								111	8		
31.12.1977	59		58								109	8		
31.12.1978	63		63								122	9		
31.12.1979	69		68								131	9		
31.12.1980	74		73								159	11		
31.12.1981	79		78								147	10		
31.12.1982	80		79								155	11		
31.12.1983	80		79								184	13		
31.12.1984	78		78								187	13		
31.12.1985	77		77								257	18	127	29
31.12.1986	78		77								357	25	157	36
31.12.1987	77		76				59	59			408	29	185	42
31.12.1988	78		78				70	70			494	35	193	44
31.12.1989	81		80				84	84			567	40	202	46
31.12.1990	87		86				84	84			462	32	226	52
31.12.1991	91		91				81	81			535	38	262	60
31.12.1992	96		95				77	77			497	35	276	63
31.12.1993	100		99				74	74			599	42	313	72
31.12.1994	104		103				73	73			619	44	320	73
31.12.1995	105		104	693		84	72	72			734	52	381	87
31.12.1996	104		103	694		84	72	72			820	58	395	90
31.12.1997	102		101	703		85	78	78			937	66	396	91
31.12.1998	101		100	757		91	89	89			1150	81	457	104
31.12.1999	101		100	829		100	100	100	101	100	1421	100	437	100
31.12.2000	101		101	893		108	117	117	107	106	1221	86	444	102
31.12.2001	101		100	993		120	130	130	112	111	1004	71	440	101
31.12.2002	101		100	1165		141	155	155	114	113	792	56	525	120
31.12.2003	99		98	1380		166	185	185	114	114	1036	73	604	138
31.12.2004	98		97	1618		195	234	234	117	116	1169	82	666	152
31.12.2005	97		96	1824		220	250	250	123	122	1258	89	620	142
31.12.2006	97		96	1990		240	239	239	125	124	1484	104	658	151
31.12.2007	97		96	2086	151	252	203	203	122	121	1589	112	730	167
31.12.2008	100		99		143	238	153	153	122	121	920	65	810	185
31.12.2009	99		99		136	228	157	157	120	119	1168	82	831	190
31.12.2010	100		99		134	223	160	160	116	115	1280	90	874	200
31.12.2011	102		102		119	198	151	151	114	114	1183	83	929	213
31.12.2012	106		105		104	173	166	165	122	121	1339	94	944	216
31.12.2013	109		108		96	160	196	195	134	133	1661	117	907	207
31.12.2014	112		111		97	162	205	205	144	143	1710	120	902	206
31.12.2015	117		116		101	169	220	220	158	157	1663	117	870	199
31.12.2016	124	100	123		106	177	232	232	170	169	1751	123	884	202
31.12.2017	130	107	132		113	189	249	249	182	181	2103	148	950	217
31.12.2018		116	143		121	202	255	254	189	188	1884	133	942	216
31.12.2019		124	153		125	209	266	266	194	193	2358	166	998	228

MSCI world Dividend Yield

Table 11: MSCI world Dividend Yield

MSCI dividend yields in % of index value from 1999 - 2019 (source: Bloomberg)

	Dividend Yield
1999	1.23
2000	1.40
2001	1.70
2002	2.23
2003	1.90
2004	1.97
2005	2.00
2006	2.06
2007	2.32
2008	3.94
2009	2.53
2010	2.40
2011	2.90
2012	2.84
2013	2.41
2014	2.49
2015	2.58
2016	2.48
2017	2.32
2018	2.73
2019	2.36

Annual Returns

Table 12: Annual Returns in Percent

Table of annual index returns in % for the four housing markets, MSCI world, and FTSE stocks

	Germany	Spain	San Diego	Dallas	MSCI world	FTSE bonds
31.12.1976	2.2%				10.3%	
31.12.1977	5.6%				-2.5%	
31.12.1978	7.3%				12.7%	
31.12.1979	8.9%				7.2%	
31.12.1980	7.4%				21.5%	
31.12.1981	7.0%				-7.9%	
31.12.1982	0.9%				5.8%	
31.12.1983	0.3%				18.6%	
31.12.1984	-2.1%				1.8%	
31.12.1985	-1.0%				37.0%	
31.12.1986	0.3%				39.1%	23.0%
31.12.1987	-0.9%				14.3%	18.4%
31.12.1988	1.7%		17.6%		21.2%	4.4%
31.12.1989	3.3%		19.7%		14.7%	4.3%
31.12.1990	7.8%		0.5%		-18.7%	12.0%
31.12.1991	4.8%		-3.2%		16.0%	15.8%
31.12.1992	5.1%		-4.7%		-7.1%	5.5%
31.12.1993	4.3%		-4.4%		20.4%	13.3%
31.12.1994	3.8%		-0.9%		3.4%	2.3%
31.12.1995	1.0%		-2.2%		18.7%	19.0%
31.12.1996	-1.3%	0.1%	0.6%		11.7%	3.6%
31.12.1997	-1.7%	1.3%	8.1%		14.2%	0.2%
31.12.1998	-1.0%	7.7%	13.8%		22.8%	15.3%
31.12.1999	0.1%	9.5%	12.6%		23.6%	-4.3%
31.12.2000	0.6%	7.7%	16.9%	5.8%	-14.1%	1.6%
31.12.2001	-0.1%	11.2%	11.1%	5.1%	-17.8%	-1.0%
31.12.2002	-0.7%	17.3%	19.4%	2.0%	-21.1%	19.5%
31.12.2003	-1.4%	18.5%	19.2%	0.2%	30.8%	14.9%
31.12.2004	-1.3%	17.2%	26.6%	2.3%	12.8%	10.3%
31.12.2005	-0.9%	12.7%	6.6%	5.0%	7.6%	-6.9%
31.12.2006	0.1%	9.1%	-4.2%	1.4%	18.0%	6.1%
31.12.2007	-0.2%	4.8%	-15.0%	-2.2%	7.1%	10.9%
31.12.2008	3.3%	-5.4%	-24.9%	0.0%	-42.1%	10.9%
31.12.2009	-0.7%	-4.3%	2.7%	-1.4%	27.0%	2.6%
31.12.2010	0.6%	-1.9%	1.8%	-3.5%	9.6%	5.2%
31.12.2011	2.4%	-11.2%	-5.3%	-1.3%	-7.6%	6.4%
31.12.2012	3.0%	-12.8%	9.4%	6.4%	13.2%	1.6%
31.12.2013	3.0%	-7.8%	18.1%	10.2%	24.1%	-4.0%
31.12.2014	2.9%	1.8%	5.0%	7.4%	2.9%	-0.5%
31.12.2015	4.6%	4.2%	7.1%	9.4%	-2.7%	-3.6%
31.12.2016	6.0%	4.5%	5.4%	7.9%	5.3%	1.6%
31.12.2017	7.4%	7.2%	7.4%	6.9%	20.1%	7.5%
31.12.2018	8.3%	6.6%	2.2%	3.9%	-10.4%	-0.8%
31.12.2019	6.8%	3.6%	4.6%	2.6%	25.2%	5.9%

Net Return after 40-year Investment

Table 13: 40-year ROI

Net return figures of the 1 M investment in the four housing markets, in stocks, and bonds in comparison to inflation. See RESULTS

Year	Germany	Spain	San Diego	Dallas	MSCI world	FTSE bonds	Inflation
0	- 0.127	- 0.111	- 0.098	- 0.098	- 0.005	- 0.005	-
1	- 0.091	- 0.053	- 0.060	- 0.031	0.062	0.034	0.019
2	- 0.053	0.008	0.011	0.040	0.134	0.075	0.039
3	- 0.014	0.074	0.088	0.117	0.211	0.118	0.060
4	0.026	0.143	0.171	0.199	0.293	0.162	0.080
5	0.069	0.217	0.260	0.288	0.381	0.208	0.101
6	0.113	0.296	0.356	0.383	0.474	0.256	0.123
7	0.159	0.381	0.459	0.485	0.574	0.306	0.145
8	0.206	0.470	0.570	0.595	0.681	0.358	0.167
9	0.256	0.566	0.690	0.713	0.794	0.412	0.190
10	0.308	0.667	0.818	0.839	0.916	0.468	0.213
11	0.362	0.775	0.957	0.975	1.045	0.526	0.236
12	0.418	0.890	1.105	1.121	1.184	0.586	0.260
13	0.476	1.013	1.266	1.277	1.332	0.649	0.285
14	0.537	1.144	1.438	1.445	1.490	0.714	0.310
15	0.601	1.283	1.623	1.626	1.658	0.782	0.336
16	0.667	1.431	1.823	1.820	1.838	0.853	0.362
17	0.735	1.589	2.038	2.028	2.030	0.926	0.388
18	0.807	1.757	2.269	2.252	2.236	1.003	0.415
19	0.881	1.936	2.517	2.492	2.455	1.082	0.443
20	0.959	2.126	2.785	2.750	2.689	1.165	0.471
21	1.040	2.329	3.073	3.026	2.938	1.250	0.499
22	1.124	2.545	3.383	3.324	3.205	1.340	0.529
23	1.211	2.775	3.716	3.643	3.490	1.432	0.558
24	1.303	3.020	4.075	3.986	3.794	1.529	0.589
25	1.397	3.281	4.461	4.354	4.118	1.629	0.620
26	1.496	3.558	4.877	4.750	4.465	1.733	0.651
27	1.599	3.854	5.324	5.174	4.835	1.842	0.683
28	1.706	4.169	5.805	5.630	5.230	1.954	0.716
29	1.818	4.504	6.322	6.120	5.652	2.071	0.750
30	1.934	4.861	6.880	6.645	6.102	2.193	0.784
31	2.055	5.242	7.479	7.210	6.583	2.319	0.818
32	2.181	5.647	8.124	7.816	7.096	2.451	0.854
33	2.312	6.078	8.818	8.467	7.645	2.588	0.890
34	2.449	6.537	9.565	9.166	8.230	2.730	0.927
35	2.591	7.026	10.369	9.917	8.855	2.878	0.964
36	2.739	7.547	11.234	10.723	9.522	3.031	1.002
37	2.893	8.102	12.164	11.589	10.235	3.191	1.041
38	3.054	8.692	13.166	12.519	10.995	3.357	1.081
39	3.221	9.321	14.244	13.517	11.807	3.530	1.122
40	3.395	9.991	15.403	14.589	12.675	3.709	1.163

Exchange Rates

Table 14: Exchange Rates EUR / USD

EUR / USD quarterly exchange rates from 1975 (calculated) to 2020, (source: Bloomberg)

Date	EUR / USD	Date	EUR / USD	Date	EUR / USD	Date	EUR / USD
31.03.75	1.36	30.03.90	1.2363	31.03.05	1.2964	31.03.20	1.1031
30.06.75	1.36	29.06.90	1.2625	30.06.05	1.2108	30.06.20	1.1234
30.09.75	1.22	28.09.90	1.338	30.09.05	1.2026	30.09.20	1.1721
31.12.75	1.24	31.12.90	1.3908	30.12.05	1.1849	18.11.20	1.1883
31.03.76	1.19	29.03.91	1.2253	31.03.06	1.2118		
30.06.76	1.18	28.06.91	1.1549	30.06.06	1.2791		
30.09.76	1.20	30.09.91	1.2544	29.09.06	1.2674		
31.12.76	1.22	31.12.91	1.3656	29.12.06	1.3197		
31.03.77	1.20	31.03.92	1.2647	30.03.07	1.3354		
30.06.77	1.21	30.06.92	1.3695	29.06.07	1.3541		
30.09.77	1.21	30.09.92	1.4284	28.09.07	1.4267		
30.12.77	1.29	31.12.92	1.2369	31.12.07	1.4589		
31.03.78	1.33	31.03.93	1.2243	31.03.08	1.5788		
30.06.78	1.31	30.06.93	1.1729	30.06.08	1.5755		
29.09.78	1.39	30.09.93	1.1892	30.09.08	1.4092		
29.12.78	1.45	31.12.93	1.1244	31.12.08	1.3971		
30.03.79	1.42	31.03.94	1.1737	31.03.09	1.325		
29.06.79	1.43	30.06.94	1.2238	30.06.09	1.4033		
28.09.79	1.50	30.09.94	1.2561	30.09.09	1.464		
31.12.79	1.51	30.12.94	1.2458	31.12.09	1.4321		
31.03.80	1.35	31.03.95	1.3615	31.03.10	1.351		
30.06.80	1.47	30.06.95	1.3605	30.06.10	1.2238		
30.09.80	1.43	29.09.95	1.3364	30.09.10	1.3634		
31.12.80	1.33	29.12.95	1.3392	31.12.10	1.3384		
31.03.81	1.22	29.03.96	1.3072	31.03.11	1.4158		
30.06.81	1.07	28.06.96	1.2809	30.06.11	1.4502		
30.09.81	1.10	30.09.96	1.2804	30.09.11	1.3387		
31.12.81	1.10	31.12.96	1.2716	30.12.11	1.2961		
31.03.82	1.01	31.03.97	1.1654	30.03.12	1.3343		
30.06.82	0.97	30.06.97	1.1255	29.06.12	1.2667		
30.09.82	0.94	30.09.97	1.1106	28.09.12	1.286		
31.12.82	0.98	31.12.97	1.0909	31.12.12	1.3193		
31.03.83	0.93	31.03.98	1.0589	29.03.13	1.2819		
30.06.83	0.89	30.06.98	1.0851	28.06.13	1.301		
30.09.83	0.85	30.09.98	1.1706	30.09.13	1.3527		
30.12.83	0.82	31.12.98	1.1736	31.12.13	1.3743		
30.03.84	0.86	31.03.99	1.0762	31.03.14	1.3769		
29.06.84	0.80	30.06.99	1.0351	30.06.14	1.3692		
28.09.84	0.73	30.09.99	1.0684	30.09.14	1.2631		
31.12.84	0.71	31.12.99	1.0062	31.12.14	1.2098		
29.03.85	0.72	31.03.00	0.9555	31.03.15	1.0731		
28.06.85	0.74	30.06.00	0.9525	30.06.15	1.1147		
30.09.85	0.82	29.09.00	0.8828	30.09.15	1.1177		
31.12.85	0.89	29.12.00	0.9427	31.12.15	1.0862		
31.03.86	0.93	30.03.01	0.8767	31.03.16	1.138		
30.06.86	0.98	29.06.01	0.849	30.06.16	1.1106		
30.09.86	1.05	28.09.01	0.9114	30.09.16	1.1235		
31.12.86	1.10	31.12.01	0.8895	30.12.16	1.0517		
31.03.87	1.16	29.03.02	0.8717	31.03.17	1.0652		
30.06.87	1.15	28.06.02	0.9915	30.06.17	1.1426		
30.09.87	1.14	30.09.02	0.9866	29.09.17	1.1814		
31.12.87	1.32	31.12.02	1.0492	29.12.17	1.2005		
31.03.88	1.26	31.03.03	1.0915	30.03.18	1.2324		
30.06.88	1.15	30.06.03	1.1512	29.06.18	1.1684		
30.09.88	1.11	30.09.03	1.1657	28.09.18	1.1604		
30.12.88	1.18	31.12.03	1.2595	31.12.18	1.1467		
31.03.89	1.11	31.03.04	1.2316	29.03.19	1.1218		
30.06.89	1.07	30.06.04	1.22	28.06.19	1.1373		
29.09.89	1.12	30.09.04	1.2436	30.09.19	1.0899		
29.12.89	1.23	31.12.04	1.3554	31.12.19	1.1213		

Index Data of eight markets (raw, normalized)

Table 15: Index Data

Normalized (1999 = 100) index data of the four initial and four additional real estate markets, MSCI world and FTSE bonds, combination of the data sets and normalization to 1999 = 100 (source: see text), additionally indicating the time frames used for calculation in this model

	Germany	Spain	San Diego	Dallas	Australia	Japan	South Africa	Brazil	MSCI world	FTSE bonds
31.12.1975	54								7	
31.12.1976	55								8	
31.12.1977	58								8	
31.12.1978	63								9	
31.12.1979	68								9	
31.12.1980	73								11	
31.12.1981	78								10	
31.12.1982	79								11	
31.12.1983	79								13	
31.12.1984	78					33			13	
31.12.1985	77					43			18	29
31.12.1986	77				44	79			25	36
31.12.1987	76		59		53	153			29	42
31.12.1988	78		70		83	134			35	44
31.12.1989	80		84		85	127			40	46
31.12.1990	86		84		84	139			32	52
31.12.1991	91		81		86	132			38	60
31.12.1992	95		77		78	113			35	63
31.12.1993	99		74		79	119			42	72
31.12.1994	103		73		93	136			44	73
31.12.1995	104	84	72		90	122			52	87
31.12.1996	103	84	72		98	101			58	90
31.12.1997	101	85	78		85	86			66	91
31.12.1998	100	91	89		85	91			81	104
31.12.1999	100	100	100	100	100	100			100	100
31.12.2000	101	108	117	106	90	87			86	102
31.12.2001	100	120	130	111	96	70	100	100	71	101
31.12.2002	100	141	155	113	125	72	70	85	56	120
31.12.2003	98	166	185	114	199	78	112	58	73	138
31.12.2004	97	195	234	116	208	81	183	81	82	152
31.12.2005	96	220	250	122	200	73	292	97	89	142
31.12.2006	96	240	239	124	233	79	318	120	104	151
31.12.2007	96	252	203	121	293	86	328	150	112	167
31.12.2008	99	238	153	121	228	95	372	215	65	185
31.12.2009	99	228	157	119	330	91	255	204	82	190
31.12.2010	99	223	160	115	392	105	333	342	90	200
31.12.2011	102	198	151	114	377	109	384	443	83	213
31.12.2012	105	173	165	121	394	96	328	459	94	216
31.12.2013	108	160	195	133	372	80	332	459	117	207
31.12.2014	111	162	205	143	364	69	288	433	120	206
31.12.2015	116	169	220	157	352	75	277	404	117	199
31.12.2016	123	177	232	169	376	79	220	267	123	202
31.12.2017	132	189	249	181	427	79	260	316	148	217
31.12.2018	143	202	254	188	366	84	299	307	133	216
31.12.2019	153	209	266	193	373	83	268	266	166	228

House price Indices of eight Markets

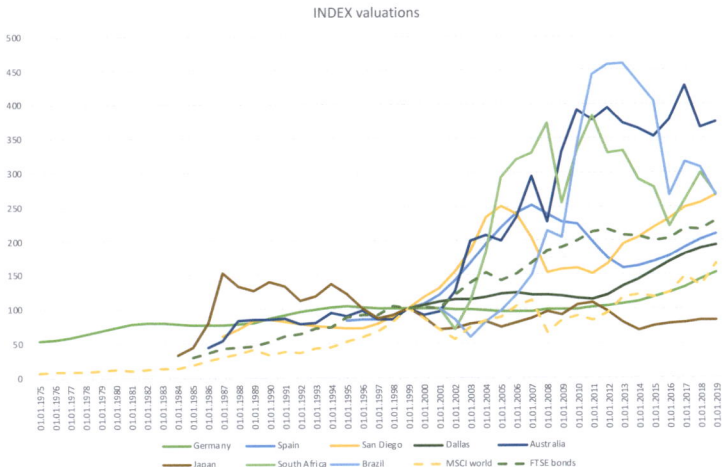

Figure 14: House Price Indices including the four additional markets, Stock and Bond Market Indices

This figure shows the normalized raw house price indices for the four areas covered (Germany, Spain, San Diego metro, and Dallas metro), as well as the MSCI world stocks and FTSE world government bonds. In addition, Brazil, South Africa, Australia and Japan are included. All data represent the raw index values from the start of each data set derived and normalized for 1999 = 100. (source: BIS, Bloomberg).

Best Practice - Process buying Real estate

The following guideline presents a step-to-step approach when considering buying real estate and lists major questions to be asked.

Knowledge of Location

Long-term owning real estate resembles having a good friend. It should be handled delicately and patiently. The first step would be assessing the own personal preferences even before focusing on potential financial returns.

- Are frequent travels pleasant (language, climate, visa-dependency, distance & access, nutrition, health aspects, crime rate, social situation)?
- Is culture, the people & the country enjoyable?
- Is the investment safe on a long-term perspective (political, legal & taxation, conflicts & wars, natural hazards, climate change)?
- Time and seasons (time zones, North vs. South hemisphere)

- Is a quiet location, an urban area or even downtown of a big city preferred?
- Are there any personal relationships?

It is adamant knowing the selection criteria. A prioritization of aspects needs to be performed to make the investment financially viable.

- Price range
- Type of real estate (single family houses, multiplexes, apartments)
- Size of the house, number of floors, style, building materials, condition
- Lot requirements (yard size, setbacks for extensions, …)
- Sunshine (orientation, shadow casted by other objects)
- Transportation (public traffic available or car dependent)?
- Noise & Pollution (traffic, children, air traffic, sewer facilities, farms, …)
- In case of remodeling: laws and restrictions
- Location & distances (shopping, schools, beach, hospital, …)

Insight to Market, Selection of Investment Properties

The desired market(s) should be continuously and retrospectively followed to monitor developments for an extended time. Whenever possible, extensive personal experience should be gained. Local media coverage can be used to learn about pending topics like crime rate or demographics (building of new schools, retirement homes, hospitals, recreation facilities, events) which may influence long-term return. The local realtor is supposed to provide additional insight while constantly keeping in mind his drive to close any sale possible. Rarely, realtors are independent from commissions like DeLeon (Realtors, 2020). A local advantage is to tour open houses extensively to get a "feeling" for the market which also helps judging the realtor's experience. Moreover, inviting a known local further steepens the learning curve. Market parameters may include:

- Median sale prices
- Average days on market
- Differences between asking and sale prices, knowing whether being in a buyer's or seller's market

- Long term growth of house values in this market, especially of the houses in focus if available
- Abnormalities compared to neighboring markets
- Local bylaws, homeowner association regulations and fees if applicable
- Property tax structure as discussed in this study

With or without a realtor the houses on market can be studied according to the criteria set and the properties of interest selected.

Using the method laid out the financial model can be developed. Depending on interest rates and credit ratings leverage or mortgage options may be considered. Unlike a stock or bond investment wiggle room needs to be taken into consideration for:

- Exceeding the original planned range of the investment for the object of desire
- Negotiated reduction of transfer pricing. However, this benefit in turn needs to be similarly accounted for when disposing of the investment
- Unplanned costs. Larger repairs may occur before reserves can be built. The model presented accounts for evenly balanced expenses on an annualized basis
- Loss in rental income due to longer lead times for finding suitable tenants
- Lower or higher actual rent than initially calculated

As an unfamiliar investor in the real estate field, it is mandatory to rely on professional help for leading through the transaction to avoid costly pitfalls. Thoroughly performed inspections of the house's condition insure against unexpected financial hurdles. It is on the investor's discretion how deep to be involved in the legal process. As with all investments basic knowledge should be obtained, especially on tax structure. Familiarizing with the HOA rules avoids legal fees and replanning costs when remodeling.

Managing the Investment

Like REITs there are two levels of continuously managing the real estate investment: the property layer and the financial aspects. Latter can be handed over to a local Certified Public Accountant (CPA) staying in close contact to the investor's own accounting environment to ensure proper filings and payments of applicable taxes.

Managing the property itself can be outsourced to a management company at a fee. Due to the rise of the internet communication and payments can be done online, especially for utilities. However, a local bank account – for a European investor in the U.S. and vice-versa - may be necessary involving extended surrounding effort to open and maintain. When renting out agents for finding and selecting tenants can be hired. These companies may combine the task of property management and renting agendas simultaneously. However, the investor has to be prepared for unusual and urgent action such as correcting errors in misaligned tax records, responding to tenants complaining (directly or via the management company) about a broken furnace, or correct mishandling of the mail by the postal service.

Summary

In contrast to buying bonds and stocks where growth can be easily monitored by reading trough the annual statements and returns from the investor's fireplace chair investing in real estate involves significant workload including continuous travels. Careful preparation during the investment process reduces the likelihood of rude awakening and therefore is adamant for any professional investor. Having finalized a solid investment of real estate, however, provides long-term satisfying peace of mind.